C++

Made Simple

Conor Sexton

Made Simple
An imprint of Butterworth-Heinemann
Linacre House, Jordan Hill, Oxford OX2 8DP
225 Wildwood Avenue, Woburn MA 01801-2041
A division of Reed Educational and Professional Publishing Ltd

Ɛ A member of the Reed Elsevier plc group

OXFORD   AUCKLAND   BOSTON
JOHANNESBURG   MELBOURNE   NEW DELHI

First published 1997
Reprinted 1998
Transferred to digital printing 2001

TRADEMARKS/REGISTERED TRADEMARKS
Computer hardware and software brand names mentioned in this book are
protected by their respective trademarks and are acknowledged

British Library Cataloguing in Publication Data
A catalogue record for this book is available from the British Library

ISBN 0 7506 3243 7

Printed in Great Britain by Antony Rowe Ltd, Eastbourne

PLANT A TREE

British Trust for
Conservation Volunteers

FOR EVERY TITLE THAT WE PUBLISH, BUTTERWORTH-HEINEMANN
WILL PAY FOR BTCV TO PLANT AND CARE FOR A TREE.

www.madesimple.co.uk

Contents

Preface

C++ Programming Made Simple is a straightforward presentation of how to write computer programs in the ANSI C++ language. It is deliberately light in tone, avoids as far as possible the more complicated parts of the C++ language and concentrates on getting aspiring C++ programmers up to speed in the shortest possible time.

The book should be suitable as an introductory guide for beginning C++ programmers and for students taking a programming course. Particularly with the latter group in mind, *C++ Programming Made Simple* presents more than 20 non-trivial and sometimes even useful exercises.

This book covers all the essentials of C++ but does not deal with the 'dark corners' of the language – for example, all the details of variable assignment and initialisation. It is not intended for experienced C++ programmers other than as a general introductory reference, or for compiler writers at all. For such readers, I recommend my own *Newnes C++ Pocket Book*, Second Edition (Butterworth-Heinemann, 1996) and (highly) *Annotated C++ Reference Manual* (Addison Wesley, 1990) by Stroustrup and Ellis.

I have not preceded the treatment of C++ with an introduction to the C subset – that would be beyond the scope of a book of this size. If you don't know at least the rudiments of C, stop now, get and read the introductory text in this series, *C Made Simple*.

When Butterworth-Heinemann asked me to do *C++ Programming Made Simple*, I became aware that the main challenge was in producing a text much lighter in weight (both literally and figuratively) than my previous C and C++ books. The priority for a *Made Simple* text is to help the reader to get the most results possible as quickly as possible and for the minimum effort expended. For this book, it means that the first chapter must take a lightning tour through only absolutely essential aspects of the C++ language, and get the reader to the point of being able to write full programs.

Chapter 2 takes the 'short path' through the rules for writing C++ classes while trying not to omit anything vital. Chapter 3 deals with class services such as overloaded operators and constructors, while Chapter 4 explains the main points of that most essential characteristic of C++, class inheritance. Chapter 5 introduces the most recent features of C++: templates, exception handling, namespaces and run-time type identification. Chapter 6 shows how to do input-output, including file I/O, from C++ programs. Each chapter presents at the end three or four practical exercises, for which full answers are given in Chapter 7.

I was enthusiastic about writing this book, which is aimed more at the novice than at the expert. I have tried to make its tone correspondingly light and its prose correspondingly simple, while hitting all the important points. I hope you find it useful.

Conor Sexton.

January, 1997.

1 A quick start with C++

Background to the C++ language

The C++ programming language is an object-oriented derivative of C. It is almost true to say that C is a subset of C++. In fact, every ISO C program written in the modern idiom (specifically, with new-style function headers) and avoiding certain C++ reserved words, is also a C++ program, although it is not object-oriented.

C++ is for technical computer programming. It can do anything that is possible with C, and then some. C++ is as suitable as C is for development of 'techie' software like operating systems, graphical interfaces, communications drivers and database managers.

C++ was developed in the early 1980s at AT&T Bell Laboratories by Dr Bjarne Stroustrup. It was originally called *C With Classes*, reflecting the fact that its major extension to the syntax of C was the implementation of the class construct.

When development of C++ began, C had been in wide use for a number of years. Certain weaknesses in C's syntax had become apparent and new techniques, especially those of object-oriented programming, could not be expressed adequately in C. In 1983, ANSI formed a technical committee, X3J11, on C language and run-time library standardisation. The ANSI C standard – American National Standard X3.159-1989 – was adopted by ANSI in 1989 and superseded in 1990 by the ISO 9899:1990 C standard. A number of early C++ innovations, especially the syntax of function prototypes, were incorporated in the (technically identical) ANSI and ISO C standards.

The first C++ 'compilers', released by AT&T, were in the form of a front-end translator, referred to as *cfront*, which converted C++ code into C. The C code was then processed to executable code by the C compiler and local loader. In 1988, the first full C++ compilers appeared; these and Integrated Development Environments (IDEs) from Borland, IBM, Microsoft and others now predominate, especially for PC and workstation environments.

Release 2.0 of C++ appeared in 1989 and was a major improvement, including most importantly, *multiple inheritance* of classes. Release 3.0 (1991) introduced *templates*. The current release is 4.0, which includes *exception-handling, run-time type identification* (RTTI) and *namespaces.* The Draft ANSI C++ Standard is based on Release 4.0 and the final ANSI C++ Standard is expected to be approved in 1997.

C++ extends C in these ways:

- It implements *objects*, defined as classes, which incorporate not just the data definitions found in C structures but also declarations and definitions of functions which operate on that data. This *encapsulation* of data and functions in a single object is the central innovation of C++.

- *Instances* of classes may automatically be initialised and discarded using *constructors* and *destructors*. This eliminates program initialisation errors.

- The way in which C++ classes are defined enforces *data hiding*; data defined in a class is by default only available to the *member functions* of that class. External, or *client*, code that uses a class cannot tamper with the internal implementation of the class but is restricted to accessing the class by calling its member functions.

- C++ allows *overloading* of operators and functions. More than one definition of a function may be made having the same name, with the compiler identifying the appropriate definition for a given function call. Ordinary operators such as '++' and '->' can also be overloaded with additional meanings.

- C++ allows the characteristics of the class type – data and functions – to be inherited by *subclasses*, also called *derived classes*, which may in turn add further data and function definitions. This encourages reuse of existing code written in the form of shareable class libraries and consequent savings in the cost of the software development process. Multiple inheritance allows derived classes to inherit characteristics from more than one base class.

- C++ allows classes to define *virtual functions*: more than one definition of a function, with the decision as to which one is selected being resolved at program run-time. This is *polymorphism*, with the run-time selection among function definitions being referred to as *late binding* or *dynamic binding*.

● *Template* classes can be defined which allow different instances of the same class to be used with data of different types but with unchanged code. This further promotes code reuse.

C++ facilities for object-oriented programming are characterised by classes, inheritance and virtual functions. These facilities make C++ particularly suitable for writing software to handle a multitude of related objects. Perhaps the most appropriate use of C++ is in implementing graphical user interfaces (GUIs), where many different but related objects are represented on a screen and are allowed to interact. Using the object-oriented approach, C++ stores these objects in class hierarchies and, by means of virtual functions, provides a generic interface to those objects (e.g. *draw object*), which saves the programmer from having to know the detail of how the objects are manipulated. This makes it easier for the programmer to develop and maintain code, as well as making the introduction of bugs into existing code less likely.

C++ has many smaller syntactic improvements over C. It provides a new reference mechanism, complementing the pointer-dereferencing approach of C. It simplifies the process of dynamically allocating and de-allocating memory, and implements a new Stream I/O library, which defines in a class hierarchy streams for input and output.

C++ is an extension of C which, by facilitating improved design practices, promises software that better reflects the real world, reduces complexity and size of code, and increases reliability.

That's enough overview stuff. Let's write our first program!

The do-nothing program

The minimal C++ program is the same as its C language counterpart. Here it is:

```
main(){}
```

This is a complete C++ program. Every C++ program must consist of one or more functions. The code shown above is a program consisting exclusively of a **main** function. Every C++ program must have one (and only one) **main** function. When it is executed, the program does nothing.

The strictly-correct C++ form of the do-nothing program is this:

```
#include   <iostream.h>
int  main(){return  0;}
```

The whole program shown is stored in a file called **donowt.cpp**.

The **.cpp** part is necessary, meaning that the file contains a C++ program; '**donowt**' is at your discretion.

iostream.h is a standard header file that contains useful declarations for compilation and execution of the program that follows. **iostream.h** is an alternative to but does not replace the C standard header file **stdio.h**. **iostream.h** declares C++ library functions and facilities (see Chapter 6); **stdio.h** does the same for Standard C Library functions such as **printf**.

The **int** (integer) preceding **main** specifies that the program returns a numeric value (in this case, zero) to the operating system when it is run. The function's parentheses are empty. This in C++ means the same as specifying a **void** argument list in C: the **main** function cannot accept any parameters.

Here is a rather complex version of the do-nothing C++ program, **donowt.cpp**. It uses a trivial C++ class to produce no output:

Do nothing

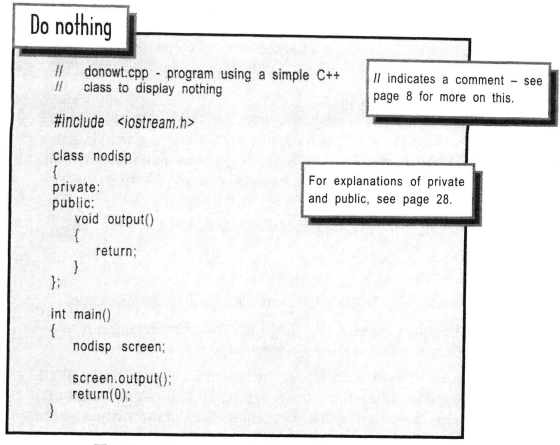

```
//    donowt.cpp - program using a simple C++
//    class to display nothing

#include <iostream.h>

class nodisp
{
private:
public:
    void output()
    {
        return;
    }
};

int main()
{
    nodisp  screen;

    screen.output();
    return(0);
}
```

// indicates a comment – see page 8 for more on this.

For explanations of private and public, see page 28.

This time, the program declares a C++ class, **nodisp**, of which the only member is a function, **output**. In the **main** function, we define an instance of the class:

```
nodisp  screen;
```

The function **nodisp::output()** (the member function output of the class **nodisp**) when executed from main with the line

```
screen.output();
```

simply returns control to the following statement. As this statement is **return(0);** at the end of **main**, **donowt.cpp** stops without making any output.

Building and running a C++ program

The filename suffix for C programs is universally **.c**. C++ filename suffixes are not so standardised. On UNIX systems, the C++ source code filename may end with either **.c** or **.C**. For many C++ systems on PCs and workstations, the suffix is **.cpp**. Some PC-based C++ compilers require the suffix **.cxx**. This book uses exclusively the suffix **.cpp**.

The **donowt.cpp** program must first be converted by compiler and linker programs into executable code. On a PC with a Borland Turbo C++ compiler and linker, you would compile **donowt.cpp** using this command-line:

```
tcc  donowt.cpp
```

This produces an output file called **donowt.exe**, which you can run at the command-line, admiring the spectacular lack of results that ensues. A similar sequence for Borland's (non-Turbo) C++ system is:

```
bcc  donowt.cpp
```

For some Microsoft C++ compilers, you can use '**c-ell**':

```
cl  donowt.cpp
```

If you're using a UNIX system, you can compile and *load* (UNIX-speak for link) the program using this command-line (note uppercase Cs):

```
CC  donowt.C
```

The executable program is in a file called **a.out** (for *assembler output*).

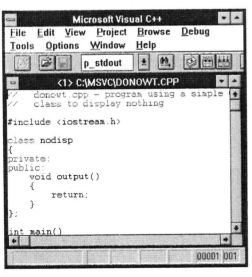

While simple programs may be built (compiled and linked) at the command-line, these days you are more likely to use an IDE (*integrated development environment*) provided by Microsoft, Borland, IBM or another supplier. Its menu-driven interface is better for managing programs of significant size. It's not the subject of this book to tell you how to use the IDEs of any software supplier.

The top-level window shown by Visual C++ running with Microsoft Windows 3.11

I assume that the information you now have will enable you to build at least simple C++ programs, and we move forward now to writing programs that actually do something. Here's one, called **message.cpp**:

```
Message

//    message.cpp - program to display a greeting
#include  <iostream.h>

int  main()
{
    cout << "Hello C++ World\n";
    return(0);
}
```

"" delimiters bounding a literal string

\n = new line character

The double-slash comment notation unofficially introduced in many C implementations is accepted in C++: all characters following the double slash // on the same line are ignored. The /*............*/ notation of C is retained in C++ but, for short comments, // is preferred.

stdio.h is replaced by the header file, **iostream.h**. This contains class and function declarations that are included by the preprocessor in the source code file and are necessary for the facilities of the C++ *Stream I/O library* to be used.

One such facility is **cout**, which is an object representing the standard output stream. The characters to the right of the << operator are sent to **cout**, which causes them to be displayed on the user's terminal screen, assuming that is the standard output device. The << operator is in fact the bitwise left-shift operator *overloaded* by the C++ system to mean 'insert on a stream'. The C++ Stream I/O system is explained in Chapter 6.

You should try entering this program at your computer and building it. As an exercise, make **message.c** display two lines:

```
Ask not what your country can do for you
Ask rather what you can do for your country
```

Here's a class-based version of **message.cpp** that produces exactly the same output as the simpler form of the program shown above:

```
//  message.cpp - uses a simple C++ class to display a greeting
#include <iostream.h>

class message
{
private:
public:
    void greeting()
    {
        cout << "Hello C++ World\n";
    }
};

int main()
{
    message user;
    user.greeting();
    return(0);
}
```

> << operator is *overloaded* by the C++ system to mean 'insert on a stream'.

Everything within the curly braces following **message** is a member of the class **message**. All the members of **message** are declared **public**; they are generally accessible. **message** only has one public member, a function called **greeting** which has no return type or argument list.

In **main**, we define an instance of the **message** class, called **user**. The **greeting** function is called and 'Hello C++ World' displayed by the call:

```
user.greeting();
```

Use of a class in this case is overkill, but from it you should be able to understand simple characteristics of the class construct.

Take note

There's much more about classes on page 14 and in Chapter 2.

9

C++ extensions to C

This section summarises the most important changes to the syntax of C++ from ISO C, other than the addition of object-oriented programming facilities and the Stream I/O, template and other libraries.

Statements

In C++, declarations do not have to come first in a function but can follow other statements:

```
#include   <iostream.h>

    int  main()
    {
        for (int  x  =  5;  x  <  10;  x++)
            ;
        cout  <<  "First declaration: "  <<  x  <<  "\n";
        int  y  =  6;
        cout  <<  "Both declarations: "  <<  x  <<  " "  <<  y  <<  "\n";
        return(0);
    }
```

> You can declare and initialise a variable as part of the controlling expression of a **for** loop.

Class and structure tags

The tag of a class, structure or enumerated type is itself a type. In C, you declare a structure like this:

```
    struct  list
    {
        int  x;
        doubley;
    };
```

and you define an instance of the structure, **inst**, like this:

```
    struct  list  inst;
```

In C++, it can be done in the same way or with the shortened form:

```
    list  inst;
```

Keywords

C++ introduces a number of new keywords, including these:

```
    class      delete     friend     inline     n e w      operator
    private    protected public      template   virtual
```

I'll explain all these later. Any C program containing any of these keywords as variable names is not a valid C++ program.

Dynamic memory allocation

As an alternative to the **malloc** and **free** function family of C, C++ introduces the **new** and **delete** operators, which perform dynamic memory allocation and deallocation like this:

```
#include  <iostream.h>
int  main()
{
    int *x;
    x = new int;
    *x = 5;
    cout << "Allocated-integer value: " << *x << "\n";
    delete x;
    return(0);
}
```

new allocates memory heap space for an integer and returns a pointer to that space to **x**. Pointer-dereferencing is used thereafter to access the contents of **x**.

Function prototypes

Although ISO C got its function prototyping mechanism from C++, there is one important difference in this respect between the two languages. In ISO C, the prototype:

```
int  myfunc();
```

means that the function **myfunc** takes zero or more parameters. In C++, it means that **myfunc** takes no parameters. This closes a loophole in ISO C type checking. Every function in a C++ program that is called before its definition *must* be declared, before the function call, with a prototype. For functions with return values of type **int**, this is unnecessary (although recommended) in ISO C.

Function call-by-reference

In C, when a variable is passed as an argument between functions, it is by default passed by value, or copied, to the called function. The variable's value in the calling function is not changed by whatever happens in the called function. To make a change to the variable have effect in the calling function, you must use a pointer to the variable as the argument in the function call. C++ additionally provides a true call-by-reference mechanism, using the *reference type*:

```
#include   <iostream.h>
void  myfunc(int&);   // prototype
int  main()
{
    int  x  =  5;
    myfunc(x);
    cout  <<  "Changed  value:  "  <<  x  <<  "\n";
    return(0);
}

void  myfunc(int&  x_ref)
{
    x_ref  =  10;
}
```

Although the initial value of **x** is 5, this is changed to **10** in **main** after the call to **myfunc**. **x** is passed to **myfunc** as a reference – **x_ref** is not a copy of or a pointer to **x** but an *alias*, or alternative name, for it. The reference is likely to be implemented internally by the C++ system with pointers and dereferencing (though the C++ specification does not require this), thus freeing the programmer from having to supply pointers as arguments and dereference them in the called function.

Inline functions

When you call an ordinary function, a jump to the function's *entry point* (address) is executed. If a function is called often, and especially if it is small, this overhead may be prohibitive. C++ provides the **inline** keyword, which is prefixed either to the function's declaration or its definition. You could declare and define the function **myfunc** in the last example as **inline** thus:

```
#include  <iostream.h>
inline  void  myfunc(int&  x_ref)  {  x_ref  =  10;  }
int  main()
{
    int  x  =  5;
    myfunc(x);
    cout  <<  "Changed  value:  "  <<  x  <<  "\n";
    return(0);
}
```

inline acts as a prompt to the compiler to treat **myfunc** as a macro: the same as if the code were embedded in the body of **main**. This avoids the function call overhead. Use of **inline** doesn't guarantee that the function will be treated as such and is, in that sense, similar to a **register** declaration. Because the **inline** function **myfunc** is defined at the place of its declaration, the function prototype may be omitted.

Operator and function overloading

C++ allows operators from its basic operator set, such as + and ==, to be given additional meanings defined by the programmer. For example, == can be used to compare structures for equality, an operation which is illegal in C. I give examples of operator overloading in Chapter 3.

You can declare and define functions more than once with different argument lists. When you call different instances of the functions, the compiler resolves the calls based on the differences between the argument lists they specify. Here are two function prototype declarations:

```
double  sqr_func(int);
double  sqr_func(float,  float);  //  overloaded
```

The function call:

```
result  =  sqr_func(1.732,  1.732);
```

causes the compiler to select the second function definition for execution.

Enough C++ to get up and running

Classes

In its fundamental extension of the capabilities of the C language, C++ introduces classes to provide language support for the object-oriented programming approach. The class is a generalisation of the structure (**struct**) construct found in C.

Like a structure, a class consists of a number of *members*. Unlike the structure, the members can be functions. You can use a class to describe a real-world object such as an insurance policy.

An insurance policy records information including the policy-holder's name and address, the policy number, the value of the entity insured and the premium to be paid for the insurance. At least four operations are possible on this information: you can open or close a policy; you can pay the premium to renew the policy; and you can make a claim. Using a C++ class, you could record the data and operations like this:

```
class policy
{
private:
    char  name[30];
    char  address[50];
    char  polno[8];
    double  ins_value;
    double   premium;
public:
    void  pol_open();
    void  pol_close();
    void  renew();
    bool  claim(double);
};
```

This is a class declaration; you can define an instance of the class – often also referred to as a *class object* or *class variable* – in a way similar to definition of a **struct** instance in C:

```
class  policy  myPolicy;
```

or

```
policy  myPolicy;
```

The second definition takes account of the fact that, in C++, the tag name, **policy**, is itself a type and that use of the **class** keyword is therefore unnecessary.

When coding the **policy** class, you would most likely store its declaration – shown above – in a header file (say, **classes.h**) #included in your program. You must then write the code of each of the class's member functions in a program file (say, **progfile.cpp**). Here's how you might define the member function **claim**:

```
bool  policy::claim(double  amount)
{
    // check  amount  of  claim  is  OK
    // pay  claim  to  policy  holder
    return(true);
}
```

The actual code of the function is unimportant, which is why it's given as comments. What is relevant here is the form of the function header:

```
bool  policy::claim(double  amount)
```

The *scope resolution operator* :: indicates that the function **claim** is a member function of the **policy** class. **claim** also returns a value of the Boolean type **bool** (only **true** and **false** values are allowable) and takes a single parameter of type **double**.

When you've declared your class and defined the code of all its member functions, the full definition of the class is complete. With an instance of the class such as **myPolicy**, you can now make the claim:

```
myPolicy.claim(1000000.0);
```

There are two parts to the class **policy**, private and public. The **private** keyword means that the class members declared following it are only accessible to member functions of the class **policy** – **pol_open**, **pol_close**, **renew** and **claim**. The **public** keyword means that any other function may make a call to any of these four functions.

The *data hiding* that is enforced by the private part of the class means that you can't access the private member functions from code other than that defined in the member functions of the **policy** class. All that is available to external, or client, code is the class's *function call* *interface*; the internal implementation of the class remains a *black box*. This mechanism results in the production of highly modular code that you and other programmers can use without having to know anything about the code other than how to call it.

The general class **policy** can be refined using derived classes that take on the characteristics of **policy** and add new ones. For example, the class **motor** might add a reserve (the unpaid first part of a claim) and a no-claims-bonus function; and the class **life** might add a term or a fixed sum assured. This is an intuitive example of class inheritance.

Constructors and destructors

In the **policy** class example, you have to remember to open and close the policy when necessary. You do this by using an instance of the class to call the **pol_open** and **pol_close** functions. A common source of errors in all programs is when initialisation such as this is omitted.

In C++, automatic initialisation and discarding are done using constructors and destructors. This makes C++ programs more reliable than their C counterparts.

A constructor is a member function of a class which initialises a variable of that class. The constructor function name is always the same as the class name. A destructor is a member function of a class which performs housekeeping operations, before the class instance is itself destroyed. The destructor function name is the same as the class name and is prefixed with a tilde, ~.

The constructor function is called as part of the definition of the class instance; the destructor is called not explicitly but automatically when the variable goes out of scope. Here is the **policy** class reworked to use constructors and destructors:

```
class policy
{
private:
    char name[30];
    char address[50];
    char polno[8];
```

```
        double   ins_value;
        double   premium;
    public:
        policy();
        ~policy();
        void  renew();
        bool  claim(double);
    };
```

The constructor function **policy()** is called automatically every time
you define an instance of the class **policy**, such as **myPolicy**. The
constructor does whatever is involved in setting up **myPolicy** as an
open policy object *immediately after* **myPolicy** is created. When
myPolicy goes out of scope, usually at the end of a function, the
destructor function ~**policy()** is automatically called. The destructor
does whatever is necessary to de-initialise the instance **myPolicy**
immediately before it is destroyed on exit from the function. Here's an
example where the constructor and the destructor are called in turn:

```
void  clientFunc()
{
    policy  herPolicy;    // define class instance
                          // also quietly call constructor policy()
        //  do some  processing
        //  destructor quietly called here to tidy up
}
```

You can specify calls to constructor functions with arguments, but
not calls to destructors. We'll see more of this in Chapter 3.

Overloading

C++ has two kinds of overloading: *function overloading* and *operator
overloading*. Below are examples of both, using the **policy** class.

● Using function overloading, you can use more than one version of
a function with the same name. The appropriate version is called
according to the parameter types used by the function.

● Using operator overloading, you can make a standard C++
operator, such as + or -, take on a new meaning.

17

Here's the **policy** class declaration changed to include an overloaded function and an overloaded operator.

```
class  policy
{
private:
    char  name[30];
    char  address[50];
    char  polno[8];
    double  ins_value;
    double  premium;

public:
    policy();
    ~policy();
    void  renew();
    void  renew(double  newPrem);
    bool  claim(double);
    bool  operator-=(double  claimAmt);
};
```

The function **renew** is overloaded. Prototypes of two versions of it are declared. The appropriate version is selected depending on the absence or presence of arguments in the function call. If you wanted to specify a non-default premium amount in renewing the policy, you could call the second **renew** member function like this:

```
myPolicy.renew(500.00);
```

The operator **-=** is overloaded, to provide an alternative way of claiming money on the policy. The keyword **operator** announces that the **-=** operator is to be given a special meaning when it is used with an instance of the class **policy**. **operator-=** is itself a function declaration, specifying a return type of **bool**.

Here are some possible definitions of the overloaded **renew** and **operator-=** functions:

```
void  policy::renew(double  newPrem)
{
    premium  =  newPrem;
}

bool  policy::operator-=(double  claimAmt)
```

```
{
    // subtract claimAmt from claim fund
    return(true);
}
```

If you call the **renew** function with one argument:

```
int main()
{
    policy.hisPolicy;
    ...
    hisPolicy.renew(250.00);
    ...
}
```

then you get the instance of the function shown above. If, on the other hand, you'd like to do a special claim, you could do this:

```
hisPolicy-=20000;  // now emigrate!!
```

When the compiler sees this special use of the -= operator, in the context of an instance of the **policy** class, it 'knows' to call the member function **operator-=** as shown above. So, although this superficially looks like a subtraction from the class instance **hisPolicy**, it's really just a call to a member function of that instance.

Inheritance

Class inheritance is one of the main characteristics of the OOP (Object Oriented Programming) approach. If you have a base class, you can also declare a derived class that takes on all the attributes of the base and adds more. The derived class is said to inherit the base class. You can build derived-class hierarchies of arbitrary depth.

Single inheritance occurs when a derived class has only one base class; multiple inheritance is when a derived class has more than one base class. You'll see multiple inheritance in Chapter 4.

Here is an example of single inheritance based on the **policy** class:

```
class policy
{
protected:
    char name[30];
```

```
    char   address[50];
    char   polno[8];
    double   ins_value;
    double   premium;
public:
    policy();
    ~policy();
    void  renew();
    void  renew(double  newPrem);
    bool  claim(double);
    bool  operator-=(double  claimAmt);
};
```

The keyword **private**, which might be expected in the base class **policy**, is instead **protected** so that its characteristics can be inherited by the derived class **motor**. Member functions of derived classes are allowed access if **protected** is used. Now you can declare the derived policy class, **motor**:

```
class  motor : public  policy
{
private:
    double   reserve;
public:
    void   no_claims_bonus();
};
```

motor inherits all non-**private** data and function members of the base class **policy**. **motor** adds the data member **reserve**. A member function of **motor** can now directly access any of the data members of **policy**. None of these data members can be accessed directly by code other than member functions of the class hierarchy. Member functions of the base class can't access members of the derived class.

motor inherits all member functions of the base class. If, in **motor**, inherited functions are redeclared, those redeclarations are said to *override* the inherited functions. Inherited functions, however, need not be overridden; they may be declared for the first time in a derived class and join inherited data and functions as members of that class.

The **main** function defines **p1** and **p2** as objects of type **policy** and **motor** respectively:

20

```
int main()
{
    policy p1;
    motor p2;
    // Calls here to 'policy' and 'motor' member functions
    return(0);
}
```

The C++ I/O system

C++ provides a complete alternative to the ISO C Standard I/O library. This is called *Stream I/O* and is based on the declarations contained in the header file **iostream.h**. This section introduces some of the simple facilities offered by Stream I/O, described further in Chapter 6.

iostream.h overloads the shift operators >> and << to be input and output operators. You can use these operators with the four standard input and output streams, which are:

cin	Standard input stream
cout	Standard output stream
cerr	Standard error stream
clog	Buffered equivalent of **cerr**, suitable for large outputs

The standard input stream typically represents the keyboard; the standard output stream the screen. **cin** is of type **istream**, a class declared in **iostream.h**. The other three streams are of type **ostream**, also declared in **iostream.h**.

If you define four variables:

```
char   c;
int    i;
float  f;
double d;
```

you can display their values by 'inserting on the output stream':

```
cout << c << i << f << d << "\n";
```

You can read from the input stream in much the same way:

```
cin >> c >> i >> f >> d;
```

Here are two examples showing some other C++ I/O facilities:

```
#include  <iostream.h>
int  main()
{
    char  c;
    while  (cin.get(c))
        cout.put(c);
    return(0);
}
```

The **get** member function of class **istream** extracts one character from the input stream and stores it in **c**. The **put** member function of class **ostream** inserts one character on the output stream.

```
#include  <iostream.h>
const  int  MAX = 80;
int  main()
{
    char  buf[MAX];
    while  (cin.getline(buf,  MAX))
    {
        int  chars_in;
        chars_in = cin.gcount();
        cout.write(buf,  chars_in);
    }
    return(0);
}
```

getline extracts at most **MAX-1** characters from the input stream and stores them in **buf**. **getline** by default finishes extracting characters after a newline is entered. The **while** loop above stops when it meets **EOF**. This is defined in **iostream.h**, and is usually represented on PCs by *Ctrl-Z*, and on UNIX by *Ctrl-d*.

gcount returns the number of characters extracted by the last call to **getline**.

write inserts up to **chars_in** characters on the output stream.

The effect of these two programs is to copy characters and strings from standard input to standard output.

Your first real C++ program

You now know enough about C++ to understand a non-trivial program and to get it working.

Here's program implemented with classes in C++ that provides a simple model of the operation of a bank account. It is organised in three files: the header file **accounts.h**; the function program file **accfunc.cpp**; and the **main** program file **accounts.cpp,** which acts as a 'driver' for the functions declared as part of the class **cust_acc**. First, the **accounts.h** header file:

accounts.h (header)

```
class  cust_acc
{
private:
    float  bal;
    int   acc_num;
public:
    void  setup();
    void  lodge(float);
    void   withdraw(float);
    void  balance();
};
```

accounts.h declares the **cust_acc** class, which has two **private** data members and four **public** member functions. The definitions of those member functions are given in **accfunc.cpp**

The **accounts.cpp** program file contains a **main** function that acts as a 'driver' of the functions declared in the class **cust_acc**. In the simulation, an account object called **a1** is created.

The function **setup** is called immediately after the creation to initialise the object in memory. This is done by prompting the program's user for initial balance and account-number values. Then, an amount of 250 is lodged to the account and 500 withdrawn. The account balance is reported after each of these operations.

accfunc.cpp (functions)

```cpp
//  Program file 'accfunc.cpp'
//  defines 'cust_acc' member functions.

#include  <iostream.h>
#include  "accounts.h"

//  customer_account  member  functions
void  cust_acc::setup()
{
    cout << "Enter number of account to be opened: ";
    cin >> acc_num;
    cout << "Enter initial balance: ";
    cin >> bal;
    cout << "Customer account " << acc_num
            << " created with balance " << bal << endl;
}

void  cust_acc::lodge(float  lodgement)
{
    bal += lodgement;
    cout << "Lodgement of " << lodgement << " accepted" << endl;
}

void  cust_acc::withdraw(float  with)
{
    if (bal > with)
    {
        bal -= with;
        cout << "Withdrawal of " << with << " granted" << endl;
        return;
    }
    cout << "Insufficient balance for withdrawal of " << with << endl;
    cout << "Withdrawal of " << bal << " granted" << endl;
    bal      = (float)0;
}

void  cust_acc::balance()
{
    cout << "Balance of account is " << bal << endl;
}
```

iostream.h is also included in **accounts.cpp**. It contains all declarations necessary to allow use of the input and output streams **cin** and **cout**. **accounts.h** is also included in both files, making the class declaration of **cust_acc** visible throughout the program.

accounts.cpp (program)

```cpp
//  Program file 'accounts.cpp'
//  drives the 'cust_acc' class


#include  <iostream.h>
#include  "accounts.h"

int main()
{
    cust_acc  a1;

    a1.setup();
    a1.lodge(250.00);
    a1.balance();
    a1.withdraw(500.00);
    a1.balance();
    return(0);
}
```

> The four member functions of the class **cust_acc** are called from **main**, in each case qualified by the class **object a1**.
> To call the functions from **main** without qualification would result in compilation errors. The data members of **cust_acc** can only be used within those functions.

The bank-account program is a very straightforward use of classes and the object-oriented programming approach. Using the Borland C++ compiler, I built it using the command-line:

    bcc accounts.cpp accfunc.cpp

producing the executable program **accounts.exe**. To execute the program, use the command-line:

    accounts

You should yourself enter and build the program. When you run it as shown, you should get results like these:

```
Enter number of account to be opened: 12345
Enter initial balance: 750
Customer account 12345 created with balance 750
Lodgement of 250 accepted
Balance of account is 1000
Withdrawal of 500 granted
Balance of account is 500
```

> User input in **bold**.

Exercises

1. Design and implement a C++ class to hold data and operations pertaining to a car object. There should be at least four data members: weight, length, colour and the maximum speed. Member functions could include start, stop and accelerate operations, as well as turn and reverse.

2. Extend the class **cust_acc** with a derived class called **savings**. This should include interest and **calc_interest** data and function members while inheriting everything in **cust_acc**. Implement the **calc_interest** function in **accfunc.cpp**.

3. Include an overloaded += operator in **cust_acc** to provide an alternative to the **lodge** function for adding money to the account's balance.

Take note

We have travelled at warp speed through the essential constructs of the C++ language. So far, I've simply not dealt with a number important aspects of C++. The focus is on rushing you along the short path to minimal competency in C++ programming. Then, you will be more ready to face the other 90% of the language. Many of the remaining concepts are, so to speak, variations on themes already stated in this chapter. The most important thing for you do to do is to 'get a handle' on the way I've presented C++ in this chapter.

2 Classes

The class construct

The C++ class construct is a generalisation of the structure, found in its original and simplest form in the C language. In C, the **struct** is an aggregation of (necessarily) data members; in C++ the **struct** may additionally have function members. The C++ **class** and **struct** are the same except that the members of the class are by default of private (restricted) access while those of the structure are public.

Let's look at an example of a class, **date**:

```
class  date
{
private:
    int  dd;
    int  mm;
    int  yy;

public:
    void  get_data();
    int    validate();
    int    find_day();
    void  disp_day(int);
};
```

You can see that some of the members of date are **private** and some are **public**. In hierarchies of derived classes (more on this in Chapter 4), you can also use the **protected** keyword.

- The *access-control* keywords **private**, **public** and **protected** may appear anywhere, in any order, between the curly braces.

- A **public** member of a class (very often a member function) can be accessed by external (client) code that is not part of the class.

- A **private** class member, on the other hand, can only be used by code defined in a member function of the same class.

If none of the access-control keywords is used in a **class** declaration, then all its members are by default **private**. In a **struct** declaration, omission of all these keywords means that all members of the structure are by default **public**. This is the only difference between the **class** and **struct** constructs in C++.

To be useful, a class must have some accessible (usually **public**) functions that may be called from client code to access indirectly the **private** data and function members of the class. The data members of the **date** class are **private**; the member functions are callable by any client code for which they are in scope.

If you don't insert the keyword **private** before the data members, they become **private** anyway, as that's the default access level for class members. If you left out *all* access specifiers, then all the members of the class would be by default **private** and the class would effectively be inaccessible and useless. Although class members are **private** by default, the preferred form is to use **private** explicitly.

You should note that my placement of all the **private** class members before the **public** ones is only my preference: the **public** members could precede the **private** ones, and **private** and **public** declarations can be intermixed.

Class instances

You define an instance of the **date** class with either of the forms:

```
class date day;
date     day;
```

and an array of class instances like this:

```
date  day_arr[20];
```

You can use the terms *class object* and *class variable* synonymously with *class instance*.

Here's how to define and initialise a pointer to the class instance **day:**

```
date  *clptr = &day;
```

Use of pointers with classes and class members is covered below (page 49).

You can't initialise a class or structure with an initialiser list in the way structures are initialised in C:

```
date  day = {1,1,97};
```

Classes and structures should be initialised with constructor functions, which you'll see in Chapter 3.

Members of a class are in *scope* for the whole outer block of the class declaration – between the curly braces. This means that member functions can directly access the other function members. If you want to get at a member function of the class variable **day** from client code, you have to do it by qualifying it with the class object **day** and the member-of (dot) operator:

```
day.get_data();
```

Within the definition of **get_data**, you can access the other members *without* qualification:

```
void   date::get_data()
{
    char c;

    cout << "Enter the day number: ";
    cin >> dd;
    cout << "Enter the month number: ";
    cin >> mm;
    cout << "Enter the year number: ";
    cin >> yy;

    // Flush the last RETURN from the input stream

    c = cin.get();
}
```

Example: the *date* class

Here's a somewhat cut-down version of the **date** class. It's organised in three files:

the header file **dates.h**;

the function program file **datefunc.cpp**;

the main program file **dates.cpp**, which calls the functions declared as part of the class **date**.

dates.h (header)

```
extern const int MINYY;
extern const int MAXYY;
extern const int MINMM;
extern const int MAXMM;
extern const int MINDD;
extern const int MAXDD;
extern const int MINFEB;
extern const int MAXFEB;
extern const int TRUE;
extern const int FALSE;

class date
{
private:
    int dd;
    int mm;
    int yy;
public:
    void get_data(); // read input date
    int  validate();  // check date for correctness
};
```

Declaration of symbolic constants used in date validation.

Declaration of shortened version of the **date** class (introduced earlier).

datefunc.cpp (functions)

```
#include  <iostream.h>
#include  "dates.h"

void  date::get_data()
{
    char c;
    cout << "Enter the day number: ";
    cin >> dd;
    cout << "Enter the month number: ";
    cin >> mm;
    cout << "Enter the year number: ";
    cin >> yy;
```

date::get_data prompts the user for input of three numbers constituting a date. I've deliberately used the form **date::get_data**. It uses the binary scope resolution operator to specify that I'm referring to the **get_data** member function of the class **date**, and not some other **get_data** function.

```
    // Flush last RETURN from the input stream

    c = cin.get();
}

int date::validate()
{
    // Validate the date according to the well-known rules

    if ((yy < MINYY) || (yy > MAXYY))
        return(FALSE);
    if ((mm < MINMM) || (mm > MAXMM))
        return(FALSE);
    if ((dd < MINDD) || (dd > MAXDD))
        return(FALSE);
    if   ((mm==4)||(mm==6)||(mm==9)||(mm==11))
        if (dd > (MAXDD - 1))
            return(FALSE);

    // If the month is February and the year is divisible evenly
    // by 4, we have a leap year, unless the year is 00.
    // 1900 was not a leap year, 2000 is

    if (mm == 2)
    {
        if (dd > MAXFEB)
            return(FALSE);
        if (((yy % 4) != 0) || (yy == MINYY))
            if (dd > MINFEB)
                return(FALSE);
    }

    // If this point is reached, we return a valid date indicator
    return(TRUE);
}
```

date::validate checks the three numbers for correctness as a date and returns **TRUE** or **FALSE** accordingly. For simplicity, the function only operates on a single century.

The header file **iostream.h** is included in both **datefunc.cpp** and **dates.cpp**. It contains, among other things, all declarations necessary to allow use of the input and output streams **cin** and **cout**, as well as the stream I/O function **get**. **dates.h** is also included in both files, making the symbolic constants and the **date** declaration visible throughout the program.

dates.cpp (program)

```cpp
#include   <iostream.h>
#include   "dates.h"

//   define global symbolic constants
const int MINYY     = 0;
const int MAXYY     = 99;
const int MINMM     = 1;
const int MAXMM     = 12;
const int MINDD     = 1;
const int MAXDD     = 31;
const int MINFEB    = 28;
const int MAXFEB    = 29;
const int TRUE      = 1;
const int FALSE     = 0;

int main()
{
    int c;
    date datein;

    // Stop user data-input when 'q'-RETURN is entered

    cout << "Press RETURN to continue, 'q'-RETURN to quit: ";
    while (c = cin.get(), c != 'q' && c != EOF)
    {
        datein.get_data();
        if ((datein.validate()) == FALSE)
            cout << "Invalid date entered\n";
        else
            cout << "Date entered is OK\n";
        cout << "Press RETURN to continue, ";
        cout << "'q'-RETURN to quit: ";
    }
    return(0);
}
```

> Definitions of the symbolic constants declared in **dates.h**

> The **main** function calls the **date** member functions

Within **main**, we define an instance **datein** of the class **date**. The two member functions of **date** are called from **main**, each prefixed by the notation **datein.**. Calls to the functions from **main** unqualified by the prefix would result in compilation errors. The data members of **date** can only be used within those functions.

The **while** loop expression is in fact two sub-expressions, related by a comma operator. We first call the input stream function **get** to extract the next user-input character from the input stream **cin**. The character assigned to **c** is compared for equality with **q** and **EOF**; if equal to either, the program stops.

The **date::get_data** function uses the extraction operator **>>** to read input from **cin**. This mechanism ignores white space and returns **EOF** if the data input does not match the type of the corresponding variable. This **EOF** is trapped by the next execution of the **while** expression.

Because white space is ignored by **cin >>**, we call the **get** function once at the end of **date::get_data** to dispose of the final **RETURN** input by the user.

Class members

Data members

You declare data members of a class within the class in the same way as ordinary (non-class-member) data objects. The class **cust_acc**:

```
class  cust_acc
{
private:
    float  bal;
    int  acc_num;
public:
    // member functions
};
```

can equally well be written:

```
class  cust_acc
{
private:
    float  bal;  int  acc_num;
public:
    // member functions
};
```

Static data members

You can't qualify declaration of class data members with any of **auto**, **register** or **extern**. If you declare a data member **static**, only one copy of that data object is allocated by the compiler in memory, regardless of how many instances of the class are defined. A static member therefore acts as a global variable within the scope of a class and might reasonably act as a global flag or counter variable. For example:

```
#include  <iostream.h>
class  run_total
{
private:
    static  int  accum;
public:
    void  increment() { accum++; }
    void  pr_total()
    {
        cout << "Accum: " << accum << "\n";
    }
};
```

```
//    definition of static member
int  run_total::accum  =  0;

int  main()
{
    run_total  total1,  total2;
    total1.increment();
    total1.pr_total();
    total2.increment();
    total2.pr_total();
    return(0);
}
```

In this program, we define two instances of the class **run_total**, **total1** and **total2**. After the first call to **increment**, the value of **accum** is **1**. After the second call to **increment** – albeit with a different class instance – the value of **accum** has become **2**.

Static data members should be defined outside the class declaration. This is the reason for inclusion of the line:

```
int  run_total::accum  =  0;
```

in global scope (outside all functions and classes). Static data members must not be initialised in this way more than once in the program.

Static data members of a class exist independently of the existence of any instances of that class: space for them is allocated at compile-time. Nevertheless, a static data member declared in this way is not a runtime definition. Additionally, although compilers often implicitly initialise such members to zero and allow their use without an explicit definition, the language specification doesn't guarantee that they will.

Nested class declarations

You can declare classes (including structures) as data members of a class. The declaration of the member class must already have been encountered by the compiler:

```
class  cust_details
{
private:
    char   accountName;
    int  age;
```

36

```
public:
    // 'cust_details' member functions
};

class  cust_acc
{
private:
    float  bal;
    int  acc_num;
public:
    cust_details  resume;
    // 'cust_acc' member functions
};
```

> The class **cust_details** is declared before an object of its type is defined in the **cust_acc** class.

function members

You can specify all the code of a member function, or just its prototype, within a class declaration. In addition, you have the option of using either of two function specifiers: **inline** and **virtual**.

If you specify a function inline as part of its declaration, the compiler is requested to expand the body of the function into the program code at the point of its call. In this way, it is treated in much the same way as a preprocessor macro: the function is expanded **inline** and the overhead of the function call is eliminated. If a class member function is *defined as part of its declaration*, it is *implicitly* **inline**:

```
class  cust_acc
{
private:
    float  bal;
    int  acc_num;
public:
    void  zero_bal()  {  bal  =  0.0;  }
    //    Other  member  functions  here
};
```

Prefixing the **inline** specifier to the function definition within **cust_acc** is unnecessary and makes no difference to the definition of **zero_bal**: You can regard the function **zero_bal** as shown as implicitly inline. You don't have to include a function's entire definition in a class declaration for the function to be inline. You can declare a member function **inline** and define it later:

37

```
class  cust_acc
{
private:
    float  bal;
    int  cust_acc;
public:
    ...
    inline  void  balance();
    ...
};
    ...
//    function  definition
void   cust_acc::balance()
{
    ...
```

A particular type of implicitly **inline** function, the *access function*, is very useful for hiding **private** member data objects. For example:

```
class  cust_acc
{
private:
    float  bal;
    int  acc_num;
public:
    int  isOverdrawn() { return(bal < 0.0); }
    //    Other  member  functions  here
};
```

Here, the Boolean value of the equality test **bal < 0.0** is returned by **isOverdrawn**. With this mechanism, you don't have to access the variable **bal** to check the customer's creditworthiness; you can instead do it with the function call:

```
    cust_acc  a1;
        ...
if  (a1.isOverdrawn())
        //    don't  give  her  the  money
```

A short function like this is particularly suitable for **inline** specification. Access functions are very common. They make it unnecessary for client code directly to access data members. The data hiding that results allows you to change the class definition while having no effect on the operation of the client code.

I'll cover virtual functions, declared with the function specifier **virtual**, in Chapter 4.

Ordinary member functions are those not specified **inline** or **virtual** and which are defined outside the class declaration. Their function headers must contain the scope resolution operator, as in the case of **balance** from the **cust_acc** class:

```
void   cust_acc::balance()
```

You can't declare a class data member twice in the same class. You *can* declare a member *function* twice in the same class but only if the two declarations have different argument lists. We'll see the rules for declaration of overloaded functions in Chapter 3. Lastly, you're not allowed declare a member data object and a member function with the same names.

Static member functions

A static member function is allowed access only the static members of its class, unless it uses a class object with one of the operators '.' or '->' to gain access. To illustrate, here's a modified version of the **run_total** example from earlier in this section:

```
#include   <iostream.h>

class  run_total
{
private:
    static int  accum;
public:
    static void  increment() { accum++; }
    void  pr_total()
    {
        cout << "Accum: " << accum << "\n";
    }
};
int  run_total::accum = 0;

int  main()
{
    run_total total1, total2;
```

```
        total1.increment();
        total1.pr_total();
        total2.increment();
        total2.pr_total();
        return(0);
    }
```

Now, as well as **accum**, the function **increment** has been declared **static** and can still access **accum**. If, however, the **static** keyword is removed from the declaration of **accum**, a compilation error results. The function **increment** can access a non-static data member of the same class by using, in this case, a class object to qualify **accum**:

```
    #include   <iostream.h>

    class  run_total
    {
    private:
        int  accum;     // non-static
    public:
        static  void  increment(run_total&  inst)
        {
            inst.accum++;   // this  usage  OK
        }
        void  pr_total()
        {
            cout << "Accum: " << accum << "\n";
        }
    };
    int  main()
    {
        run_total  total1,  total2;

        total1.increment(total1);
        total1.pr_total();
        total2.increment(total2);
        total2.pr_total();
        return(0);
    }
```

In the examples above, you should note that the static member function **increment** can be used without reference to instances of the class **run_total**:

40

```
int main()
{
    run_total total1, total2;

    run_total::increment();
    total1.pr_total();
    run_total::increment();
    total2.pr_total();
    return(0);
}
```

Here, only access to the non-static function **pr_total** must be controlled by the class instances **total1** and **total2**.

Example: using static class members

As a more practical example of a case in which static class members might be used, here's the bank-account example from Chapter 1 reworked so that the account number is no longer prompted for in the **setup** function. Instead, each time you create an account instance, the next available number is 'peeled off'.

In summary, you need a variable global to all **cust_acc** class instances to hold information logically common to them all.

accounts.c (header)

```
class cust_acc
{
private:
    float bal;
    static int acc_num;
    int my_acc_num;
public:
    void setup();
    void lodge(float);
    void withdraw(float);
    void balance();
};
```

accfunc.cpp (functions)

```cpp
//  defines cust_acc member functions

#include  <iostream.h>
#include  <string.h>
#include  "accounts.h"

//  only setup function has changed
void  cust_acc::setup()
{
    my_acc_num = acc_num++;
    cout << "Enter opening balance for account "
            << my_acc_num << ": ";
    cin >> bal;
    cout << "Customer account " << my_acc_num
            << " created with balance " << bal << endl;
}
```

> Get 'next' account number stored in static variable **acc_num**

account.cpp (program)

```cpp
#include  <iostream.h>
#include  "accounts.h"

int cust_acc::acc_num = 1000;

int main(void)
{
    cust_acc a1;
    a1.setup();
    a1.lodge(250.00);
    a1.balance();
    a1.withdraw(500.00);
    a1.balance();

    cust_acc a2;
    a2.setup();
    a2.lodge(1000.00);
    a2.balance();
    a2.withdraw(300.00);
    a2.balance();
    return(0);
}
```

> 'first' account number set here – add 1 for every account created

Friends

In a strict object-oriented programming world, only public member functions of a class are allowed direct access to the private member variables. Things are not that simple, however, and C++ provides the **friend** mechanism, which allows the rules to be bent.

A function may be specified within a class declaration and prefixed with the keyword **friend**. In such a case, the function is *not* a member of the class, but the function is allowed access to the private members of the class.

Here's the **cust_acc** class containing a **friend** declaration:

```
class  cust_acc
{
private:
    float  bal;
    static  int  acc_num;
    int    my_acc_num;
public:
    void   setup();
    void   lodge(float);
    void   withdraw(float);
    void   balance();
    friend  void  enquiry();
};
```

The function **enquiry** is not a member of the class, but you can call it from anywhere else in the program and it nevertheless has full access to all members of **cust_acc**, even the private ones.

Take note

You're encouraged to be sparing in your use of **friend** declarations. Too many friends can be a bad thing. A case where **friends** are useful, even necessary, is that of operator overloading, of which more in the next chapter.

Class scope

Every C++ data object has local, function, file or class scope. Scope defines the visibility of a data object.

- If it has file scope, it's visible throughout the program file in which it is defined and is said to be global.

- If a data object has function scope, it is visible only in the function in which it is defined. Only **goto** labels have function scope.

- If a data object has local scope, its visibility is confined to the local enclosing compound statement.

Each of file, function and local scope are part of the C language and have been incorporated in C++. Class scope is added by C++.

A C++ class has its own scope. This means that a class member is directly visible only to member functions of the same class. Access to the class member is otherwise limited to cases where the member-of (.), pointer (->) and scope-resolution (::) operators are used with either the base class or a derived class. A data object declared as a **friend** of a class belongs to that class's scope.

Here's a modified example of the **date** class, which illustrates the different aspects of class scope:

```
class  date
{
private:
    int  dd;
    int  mm;
    int  yy;
public:
    void  get_data();
        { cin >> dd >> mm >> yy; }        // inline
    int    validate();
    int    find_day();
    void  disp_day(int);
};
```

In client code, such as the **main** function, we define an instance of the class and a pointer to it:

```
date    day;
date    *dptr = &day;
```

For all of the four member functions, all other class members are in scope. Thus, the code of the **validate** function might, if necessary, call the function **disp_day**, even though **disp_day** is declared later in the class than **validate**. Member function code may access other class members – data and function – directly, without using any prefixes to resolve scope.

To access function members from client code, you must use the member-of and pointer operators:

```
day.dd
dptr->dd
```

Likewise:

```
day.validate()
```

is equivalent to:

```
dptr->validate()
```

If you don't use these prefixes, the members are out of scope for the client code and compilation errors result. The **private** class members are always out of scope for client code; you can only access them indirectly using member functions, for which they are in scope.

To see the effect of the scope resolution operator, let's look at a modified version of the **run_total** example from page 39:

```
#include   <iostream.h>

class  run_total
{
private:
    static  int  accum;
public:
    static  void  increment()  {  accum++;  }
    void  pr_total()
    {
        cout  <<  "Accum:  "  <<  accum  <<  "\n";
    }
};

int  run_total::accum  =  0;
int  main()
```

```
{
    run_total total1, total2;
    int run_total = 11;

    run_total::increment();
    total1.pr_total();
    run_total::increment();
    total2.pr_total();
    cout << run_total << "\n";
    return(0);
}
```

Here, although the class name, **run_total**, is redefined as an integer in **main**, class scope is *resolved* in the calls to the static member function **increment**, by means of the binary scope resolution operator. The result of the program is:

```
Accum: 1
Accum: 2
1 1
```

With derived classes and nested classes, use of the scope resolution operator is at times necessary to avoid ambiguity when accessing class members. Otherwise, it's best to avoid masking declarations in this way: it doesn't help program reliability or readability.

Nested class declarations

Where a class is declared in class scope, the declaration is said to be nested – one class is declared within another. Declarations made in the nested class are not in scope for functions in the enclosing class and must be accessed according to the normal procedures. Equally, declarations in the enclosing class are not in scope for functions declared in the nested class.

Here are the relevant parts of an example program, again based on the **date** class, that shows use of nested classes:

```
// file 'dates.h', contains nested classes 'date' and 'curr_time'

class date
{
private:
```

```
        int  dd;
        int  mm;
        int  yy;
    public:
        class  curr_time
        {
        private:
            int  hr;
            int  min;
            int  sec;
        public:
            void  correct_time();
        }t;

        void  get_data();
        int   validate();
        int   find_day();
        void  disp_day(int);
    };
```

> Nesting classes in C++ is the same as nesting structures in C, with the obvious extension of function as well as data members.

The nested class **curr_time** is added to the **date** class. **curr_time** is declared and an instance of it defined within **date**.

In this case, the function **correct_time** is used to reset the data members of class **curr_time**, probably by calling library functions declared in the standard header file **time.h**.

The calling sequence for this function is:

```
    date  day;

        ...

    day.t.correct_time();    // set correct time
```

To conform with the C++ scope rules, you must write the header of the **correct_time** function like this:

```
    void   date::curr_time::correct_time()
```

The definition of an instance of the class **date** also defines an instance of **curr_time** because of the definition of t embedded in **date**. The members of a nested class are not in scope for those of the enclosing class; to qualify the function header of **correct_time** only with the scope resolution **date** would cause the function **correct_time** to be out of scope even though it is a member of a class nested within **date**.

The ANSI C++ standard has introduced an extension allowing forward declaration of nested classes. In the example above showing the **curr_time** class nested within **date**, a forward declaration of **curr_time** can instead be used with ANSI C++ implementations:

```
class date
{
private:
    int dd;
    int mm;
    int yy;
public:
    class curr_time;
    curr_time t;
    void get_data();
    int   validate();
    int   find_day();
    void disp_day(int);
};

class curr_time
{
private:
    int hr;
    int min;
    int sec;
public:
    void correct_time();
};
```

Classes and pointers

You can use pointers to classes in C++ in much the same way as you use structure pointers in C. C++ adds the reference notation and a special set of operators for use with pointers to class members. Let's look at this simple class declaration:

```
#include  <iostream.h>
class  fraction
{
public:
    double  f;
    double  g;
};
```

The **main** function following defines two instances of the class, **x** and **y**, and a pointer to a double floating-point type. The pointer is used in the conventional way to access and display the members of both instances of the class.

```
int  main()
{
    fraction  x,  y;
    double  *dptr;

    x.f  =  1.1;
    y.f  =  2.2;
    x.g  =  3.3;
    y.g  =  4.4;

    dptr  =  &x.f;
    cout  <<  *dptr  <<  "\n";
    dptr  =  &y.f;
    cout  <<  *dptr  <<  "\n";
    dptr  =  &x.g;
    cout  <<  *dptr  <<  "\n";
    dptr  =  &y.g;
    cout  <<  *dptr  <<  "\n";
    return(0);
}
```

The displayed results of the program are:

```
1.1
2.2
3.3
4.4
```

Class member pointers

It's OK to use pointers to class members in the way shown above. But C++ provides an alternative type of pointer, the pointer to a class member, specially for accessing class members. Here's the same example reworked to illustrate it:

```cpp
#include  <iostream.h>
class  fraction
{
public:
    double  f;
    double  g;
};

int  main()
{
    fraction  x,  y;
    double   fraction::*dptr;

    x.f  =  1.1;
    y.f  =  2.2;
    x.g  =  3.3;
    y.g  =  4.4;

    dptr  =  &fraction::f;
    cout  <<  x.*dptr  <<  " "  <<  y.*dptr  <<  "\n";

    dptr  =  &fraction::g;
    cout  <<  x.*dptr  <<  " "  <<  y.*dptr  <<  "\n";
    return(0);
}
```

The line:

```cpp
double   fraction::*dptr;
```

defines **dptr** not just as a pointer to an object of type **double**, but specifically as a pointer to **double** members of **fraction** objects. You can't later use the member pointer **dptr** to point to a simple **double** data object. The pointer is then assigned the address of the member variable **f** in class **fraction**. This notation is used to access **x.f**:

```cpp
x.*dptr
```

You can read the operator **.*** (introduced with C++) as *x-dot-pointer-to-f*; returns the same value as **x.f**. Unlike the use of conventional pointers, the pointer **dptr** is used without change to access the member **f** of the **y** instance of the class; the notation used is **y.*dptr**. This time, the displayed results are:

```
1.1  2.2
3.3  4.4
```

You can use the **->*** operator (also introduced with C++) instead of the **.*** operator. Suppose that pointers to the class instance, rather than the class instance itself, are used:

```
fraction *xptr = &x;
fraction *yptr = &y;
```

The first display command reads:

```
cout << xptr->*dptr << " " << yptr->*dptr << "\n";
```

Member function pointers

Use of the specialised pointer-to-class-member syntax may be desirable in all cases where class members are to accessed using pointers but you must use it where a member function is to be called with a pointer. You can't access member functions of a class using conventional function pointers. For example, a conventional pointer to function returning integer:

```
int (*fptr)();
```

can't be used to point to a member function of a class, even if that function exactly matches the pointer definition in signature.

Consider the **coord** class with a function member:

```
class coord
{
private:
    int x_coord;
    int y_coord;
public:
    int locate_coords();
};
```

You can't use a conventional function pointer to point to the function **locate_coords**. Instead, we define a pointer to member function:

```
int (coord::*mem_fn_ptr)();
```

assign a function address to it like this:

```
mem_fn_ptr  =  coord::locate_coords;
```

and call it:

```
mem_fn_ptr();
```

Use of the member-pointer operators provides better control than using ordinary pointers to point to members and less likelihood of pointers being used for unintended purposes. Unfortunately, the syntax is somewhat complicated. This may encourage programmers to stick where they can with traditional pointers and (as even C programmers are inclined to do) avoid function pointers altogether.

Classes as function arguments

Pointers to classes are sometimes used where classes instances are being passed as arguments to functions. In C++, you usually use *reference declarations* instead to achieve the same purpose:

```
#include  <iostream.h>

class  fraction
{
public:
    double  f;
    double  g;
};

void   change_class(fraction&);        Function  prototype  with
                                       reference   argument
int  main()
{
    fraction  x, y;
    double   fraction::*dptr;
    x.f  =  1.1;
    y.f  =  2.2;
    x.g  =  3.3;
    y.g  =  4.4;

    change_class(x);
```

```
    dptr  =  &fraction::f;
    cout  <<  x.*dptr  <<  " "  <<  y.*dptr  <<  "\n";

    dptr  =  &fraction::g;
    cout  <<  x.*dptr  <<  " "  <<  y.*dptr  <<  "\n";
    return(0);
}

void  change_class(fraction&  xptr)
{
    xptr.f  =  5.5;
    xptr.g  =  6.6;
}
```

When you run the program, you get this result:

```
5.5  2.2
6.6  4.4
```

Depending on how it implements the C++ language, the compiler may replace the reference code with pointer referencing and de-referencing syntax. In any event, you're saved from having to do it. The reference (trailing **&**) is only referred to in the **change_class** prototype and function header; in **change_class**, the class members are accessed as if the function had been called by value with the argument **x**.

Reference declarations qualified **const** are strongly recommended if you don't want a called function to change the value of its parameter:

```
void  dont_change_class(const  fraction&  xptr)
{
    //  compile error if  x   members changed
}
```

You can suffix a function itself with **const**:

```
class  fraction
{
    //
public:
    dont_change_members()    const
    {
        // function  code  here
    }
};
```

const functions generate compilation errors if they attempt to change the value of the class object members with which the function is called. The **const** suffix only has meaning for class member functions.

The this pointer

Every member function of a class has an implicitly defined constant pointer called **this**. The type of **this** is the type of the class of which the function is member. It's initialised, when a member function is called, to the address of the class instance for which the function was called.

Here's a representative example of the use of **this**:

```cpp
#include  <iostream.h>

class  coord
{
private:
    int  x_coord,  y_coord;
public:
    void  set_coords(int  x_init,  int  y_init)
    {
        x_coord  =  x_init;
        y_coord  =  y_init;
    }
    void  change_coords(int,  int);
    void   display_coords()
    {
        cout  <<  "Coordinates:  "  <<  x_coord
              <<  " "  <<  y_coord  <<  "\n";
    }
};

int  main()
{
    coord  c1;

    c1.set_coords(5,  10);
    cout  <<  "Original  C1"  <<  "\n";
    c1.display_coords();
    c1.change_coords(15,  20);
```

```
        cout << "Changed C1" << "\n";
        c1.display_coords();
        return(0);
}

void coord::change_coords(int x_chg, int y_chg)
{
        coord c2;

        c2.set_coords(x_chg,  y_chg);
        cout << "Display C2" << "\n";
        c2.display_coords();

        *this = c2;
}
```

The program produces these results:

```
Original C1
Coordinates: 5  10
Display C2
Coordinates: 15  20
Changed C1
Coordinates: 15  20
```

The **this** pointer is useful when, during execution of a class member function, you want to get a 'handle' on the class object used to call the function. Because, in a member function, the class variable with which the function was called is out of scope, the **this** pointer is provided as that 'handle'.

Whether or not the **this** pointer is explicitly used in class member functions, the C++ compiler accesses all class members using an implicit **this** pointer.

Static member functions do not have **this** pointers. There is only one instance of a static member function for a class, so use of **this** does not make much sense. Any attempt to use this in a static member function causes a compilation error. Static member functions may otherwise be accessed by means of pointers using the same syntax as non-static member functions.

Exercises

1. Given the abstract object *clock*, identify attributes of the class **clock**. Declare **clock** as a C++ class. Ensuring that the class contains at least one member function, write down the definitions (as they would be written in a separate **.cpp** file) of each of the functions and show how they would be called from an external function such as **main**.

2. Given the class declaration:

```
class policy
{
private:
    char  name[30];
    char  address[50];
    char  polno[8];
    double  ins_value;
    double  premium;
public:
    void  pol_open();
    void  pol_close();
    void  renew();
    bool  claim(double);
};
```

    what is wrong with this definition of an instance:

```
policy jsmith =
        {"J.  Smith","Valley  Road","12345678",1000.00,100.00};
```

    Why? How should it be done?

3. Change the **policy** class as it appears in 2 above so that each instance of the class takes its policy number from a static member **glob_polno**. Initialise **glob_polno** appropriately to a value of **10000**. Create at least two instances of **policy** and demonstrate that they have been set up with different policy numbers.

3 Class services

Introduction

This chapter describes the facilities provided by C++ to allow you to work with class instances without having to know what's inside. For example, suppose we had an instance, **A1**, of the bank-account class **cust_acc**. We might want to transfer the account to **A2**. The instance-level assignment:

```
A2 = A1;
```

is much nicer and more intuitive than 'reaching inside' the instances and copying the members one-by-one. We might want to create a new account **A3** and set it up initially with the contents of **A2**:

```
cust_acc  A3(A2);
```

and for this we need a *copy constructor*. We might want, at the instance level, to add money (pounds, dollars, euros, whatever) to the account. It would be attractive to be able to write:

```
A3++;
```

to add one pound, or

```
A3+=5;
```

to add five dollars. These are two cases of overloaded operators.

This chapter, in essence, concerns itself with constructors and overloaded operators. It describes how you can use these two C++ language facilities to work with classes at the instance level, without having to be aware of the internals. Step into the shoes of the C++ programmer who *uses* classes defined and implemented by others, and these high-level facilities make life a whole lot simpler. Put on your class designer's hat, on the other hand, and you find that you have to know how to use these facilities in order to hide the details from the programmers who will be using *your* classes.

Constructors, destructors, overloaded operators and, especially, their side-effects, are not simple. But, this book is a *Made Simple* so what follows is the 'short path': a straightforward presentation of the essentials. If you want to get into the 'dark corners' look beyond this book to my other publication, the *Newnes C++ Pocket Book*, or the *Annotated C++ Reference Manual (ARM)* by Stroustrup and Ellis.

Constructors and destructors

When you define a variable in C, you have no automatic mechanism for ensuring that the variable is set to some reasonable value when it is created or that the variable is 'tidied up' (for example, its memory deallocated) immediately before it is destroyed.

Constructor and destructor functions are introduced in C++ for this purpose. Both are (and must be) class member functions that have the same name as the class of which they are a part. In the case of the destructor, the name is prefixed with a tilde '~'.

Here's an abstract example that has the single virtue of being short:

```
class  newclass
{
private:
    //    private data members defined here
    ...
public:
    newclass()                      // constructor function
    {
        // initialising statements here
        cout  <<  "Constructing....\n";
    }
    //    other public members defined here
    ...
    ~newclass() //destructor  function
    {
        // un-initialising statements here
        cout  <<  "Destructing....\n";
    }
};
```

Here, the constructor function **newclass** is defined as a public member function of the class of the same name. You don't have to make a constructor **public**; it can be **private** or **protected** and it can be anywhere in the list of member functions. Similarly, the destructor function **~newclass** need not be declared **public** and may be declared anywhere among other declarations.

Note that constructors and destructors are usually declared with **public** access. If **private**, they are more difficult to use because access to them is restricted to member functions of the same class.

When you define an instance of **newclass**:

```
newclass   nc;
```

the initialising statements in the body of the **newclass** constructor function are executed. When **nc** goes out of scope, the destructor function **~newclass** is implicitly called and its uninitialising statements do suitable tidying-up operations, which usually include returning storage to the system's free list.

A destructor is almost always called implicitly in this way. You will very rarely, if ever, explicitly call a destructor function.

Constructor functions do not create class objects, nor do destructor functions destroy them. A class object is created when you define it; creation is *immediately followed* by execution of the body of the constructor function. When a class object goes out of scope, its destructor function is executed *and only then* is the object destroyed.

Let's see how these functions are called. First, the declaration of **newclass**:

```
class  newclass
{
private:
    int  a,  b,  c;
public:
    newclass()
    {
        a = b = c = 0;
        cout  <<  "Constructing....\n";
    }
    ~newclass()
    {
        cout  <<  "Destructing....\n";
    }
};
```

Next, here are the functions that use **newclass**:

```
int  main()
{
    newfunc();
    return(0);
}
```

```
void  newfunc()
{
    newclass  nc1;
    {
        cout  <<  "Defining   nc2....\n";
        newclass  nc2;

    }
    cout  <<  "Out  of  scope  of   nc2....\n";
}
```

newclass has three data members, all integers, and two member functions, its constructor and destructor. The constructor sets the three integers to zero and displays a message. The destructor simply displays a message. In the function **newfunc**, two instances, **nc1** and **nc2**, of **newclass** are defined. The definitions call the constructor; when the definitions go out of scope, the destructor is implicitly called.

The displayed output of the program is this:

```
Constructing....
Defining   nc2....
Constructing....
Destructing....
Out  of  scope  of   nc2....
Destructing....
```

Constructor and destructor functions must not have return types, not even **void**. They may contain **return** statements but when **return** is used in this way it must have no operands. Only **return;** is valid. Constructors may take parameters; destructors must not, although **void** may be specified as a destructor argument list.

Simple constructor example

Here, once again using the bank-account class example, is a simple use of constructors. In previous declarations of **cust_acc**, we've used the member function **setup** to initialise the data members. This means that, after defining an instance of **cust_acc**, you must remember to call **setup** to do the initialisation. In the next example, we replace this two-step procedure with a constructor. A destructor is also included, in

61

this case mainly for illustration. The reworked **cust_acc** class is declared in the **accounts.h** header file:

accounts.h (header)

```
class  cust_acc
{
private:
    float  bal;
    int  acc_num;
public:
    cust_acc();
    void  lodge(float);
    void  withdraw(float);
    void  balance();
    ~cust_acc()
    {
        cout  <<  "Account "  <<  acc_num  <<  " closed"  <<  endl;
    }
};
```

accfunc.cpp contains the definitions of the class member functions other than the destructor. These definitions are unchanged from the examples in Chapter 2, except that **setup** is replaced by a constructor.

Immediately after you define in memory the **cust_acc** instance, **a1**, the constructor function **cust_acc::cust_acc()** is automatically called to perform initialising operations on **a1**.

The creation of the **a1** object:

```
cust_acc  a1;
```

is therefore also an implicit function call that replaces the previous explicit call to **setup**.

At the end of **main**, when the object **a1** goes out of scope, the destructor function **cust_acc::~cust_acc** is quietly called and 'closes' the account **a1**.

```cpp
#include  <iostream.h>
#include  "accounts.h"

//
//  customer_account  member  functions
//
cust_acc::cust_acc()
{
    cout << "Enter number of account to be opened: ";
    cin >> acc_num;
    cout << "Enter initial balance: ";
    cin >> bal;
    cout << "Customer account " << acc_num
              << " created with balance " << bal << endl;
}

void cust_acc::lodge(float  lodgement)
{
    bal += lodgement;
    cout << "Lodgement of " << lodgement  << " accepted" << endl;
}

void cust_acc::withdraw(float  with)
{
    if (bal > with)
    {
        bal -= with;
        cout << "Withdrawal of " << with << " granted" << endl;
        return;
    }
    cout << "Insufficient balance for withdrawal of "  << with << endl;
    cout << "Withdrawal of " << bal << " granted" << endl;
    bal       = (float)0;
}

void  cust_acc::balance()
{
    cout << "Balance of account is " << bal << endl;
}
```

```
#include   <iostream.h>
#include   "accounts.h"

int  main()
{
    cust_acc  a1;

    a1.lodge(250.00);
    a1.balance();
    a1.withdraw(500.00);
    a1.balance();
    return(0);
}
```

The constructor is declared in the class definition and defined later in the **accfunc.cpp** program file with this header:

```
cust_acc::cust_acc()
```

In other functions that are not constructors, you must specify a return type at the start of the function header. With constructors and destructors, you must not. When you run the program, its output looks like this (user-entered stuff is in **bold**):

```
Enter number of account to be opened: 12345
Enter initial balance: 1000.00
Customer account 12345 created with balance 1000
Lodgement of 250 accepted
Balance of account is 1250
Withdrawal of 500 granted
Balance of account is 750
Account 12345 closed
```

Constructors taking parameters

Constructors are functions and can take parameters like any other function. This class uses a constructor function taking parameters:

```
#include  <iostream.h>

class  coord
{
private:
    int  x_coord, y_coord;
public:
    coord(int  x, int  y)
    {
        x_coord = x;
        y_coord = y;
    }
    void  print()
    {
        cout << x_coord << "\n";
        cout << y_coord << "\n";
    }
};

int  main()
{
    coord  point1  =  coord(5,10);

    point1.print();

    //   coord  point2;          // illegal

    coord   point3(15,20);      // abbreviation

    point3.print();
    return(0);
}
```

This program illustrates several aspects of constructor parameter syntax. The constructor function **coord** – defined in full in the class and therefore implicitly **inline** – takes two integer parameters. From the code in **main**, you can see two ways of calling **coord**. The first:

```
coord  point1  =  coord(5,10);
```

is the full version; the function **coord** is called with the arguments **5** and **10** and the results of this function – the variables **x_coord** and **y_coord** set to **5** and **10** respectively – are assigned to **point1**, which is an instance of **coord**. The second constructor calling sequence:

```
coord   point3(15,20);
```

is an abbreviation equivalent to the definition and initialisation of **point1** above. You will usually use this abbreviated form of definition and constructor call in preference to the full version.

The simple definition in the last section:

```
cust_acc   a1;
```

invokes the constructor **cust_acc::cust_acc**, which does not take parameters. By contrast, the (commented out) definition of **point2** is illegal: you can't call a constructor that takes parameters with no argument list. The correct forms are the definitions of **point1** and **point3**. The result of the program is simple:

```
5
10
15
20
```

There is no destructor function in the class **coord**. You'll use destructors most often when a member function – usually the constructor – performs dynamic allocation of memory that should be freed at or before the end of program execution. In this case, no memory is dynamically allocated. You'll see constructors with dynamic allocation later in this chapter.

Example: constructors taking parameters

Here's a more substantial example of use of constructors – with and without parameters – in the familiar **cust_acc** class.

The **cust_acc** class declaration now has two constructor functions. The first is a simple setup of objects of the **cust_acc** class using prompts, as earlier. The second is an *overloaded constructor*.

```
cust_acc::cust_acc(int  num_init, float  bal_init)
```

causes a new instance of the class **cust_acc** to be assigned the values specified by the two variables in the argument list.

accounts.h (header)

```cpp
class cust_acc
{
private:
    float bal;
    int  acc_num;
public:
    cust_acc();
    cust_acc(int, float);
    void lodge(float);
    void withdraw(float);
    void balance();
};
```

Overloaded constructor

accfunc.cpp (functions)

```cpp
#include  <iostream.h>
#include  "accounts.h"

cust_acc::cust_acc()
{
    cout << "Enter number of account to be opened: ";
    cin >> acc_num;
    cout << "Enter initial balance: ";
    cin >> bal;
    cout << "Customer account " << acc_num
         << " created with balance " << bal << endl;
}

cust_acc::cust_acc(int num_init, float bal_init)
{
    acc_num = num_init;
    bal = bal_init;
    cout << "Customer account " << acc_num
         << " created with balance " << bal << endl;
}

void cust_acc::lodge(float lodgement)
{
    bal += lodgement;
    cout << "Lodgement of " << lodgement << " accepted" << endl;
}
```

This is a special case of
an overloaded function –
see later in this chapter.

67

```
void  cust_acc::withdraw(float  with)
{
    if (bal > with)
    {
        bal -= with;
        cout << "Withdrawal of " << with << " granted" << endl;
        return;
    }
    cout << "Insufficient balance for withdrawal of " << with << endl;
    cout << "Withdrawal of " << bal << " granted" << endl;
    bal        = (float)0;
}

void  cust_acc::balance()
{
    cout << "Balance of account is " << bal << endl;
}
```

accounts.cpp (program)

```
#include  <iostream.h>
#include  "accounts.h"

int  main()
{
    cust_acc a1;
    a1.lodge(250.00);
    a1.balance();
    a1.withdraw(500.00);
    a1.balance();
    cust_acc a2(12345, 1000.00);
    a2.balance();
    a2.withdraw(750.00);
    a2.balance();
    return(0);
}
```

In **main**, you create instances, **a1** and **a2**, of type **cust_acc**. **a1** is initialised by the constructor function **cust_acc::cust_acc()**, the *default constructor*. This prompts the user for input of the account number and opening balance, confirming that the account has been

68

successfully opened. Definition of **a2** causes the constructor with the argument list to be called. The variable members of **a2** are assigned the argument values within that constructor. Here's the output of the program as I tested it:

```
Enter number of account to be opened: 12345
Enter initial balance: 2000.00
Customer account 12345 created with balance 2000
Lodgement of 250 accepted
Balance of account is 2250
Withdrawal of 500 granted
Balance of account is 1750
Customer account 12345 created with balance 1000
Balance of account is 1000
Withdrawal of 750 granted
Balance of account is 250
```

Constructors and dynamic memory allocation

You can use constructors to initialise class objects for which memory has been dynamically allocated by the **new** operator:

```
#include  <iostream.h>

class  coord
{
private:
    int  x_coord,  y_coord;
public:
    coord(int  x,  int  y)
    {
        x_coord  =  x;
        y_coord  =  y;
    }
    void  print()
    {
        cout  <<  x_coord  <<  "\n";
        cout  <<  y_coord  <<  "\n";
    }
};
```

```
int  main()
{
    coord  *p_coord;

    p_coord  =  new  coord(5,10);

    p_coord->print();
    return(0);
}
```

Here, a new instance of the class type **coord** is allocated and its memory address assigned to the pointer **p_coord**. Additionally, the class's constructor function is called, initialising the data members of the class to the values **5** and **10**.

A class object represented by an automatic variable is destroyed when that variable goes out of scope. On the other hand, a class object for which memory is dynamically allocated:

```
class  coord
{
    //
};

ptr  =  new  coord;
```

is persistent. When **ptr** goes out of scope, its destructor isn't called and the memory associated with **ptr** remains allocated. For the destructor to be invoked, you must explicitly deallocate the memory:

```
delete  ptr;
```

for the destructor to be implicitly called.

Function overloading

C++ introduces overloaded functions. You can use a single function name to refer to more than one instance of the function, with each instance of the function having different argument lists. The compiler discriminates between function instances using the different argument lists in their prototypes. Overloaded constructors, introduced later in this chapter, are a special case of overloaded functions.

Function overloading give you flexibility: you can use the same function name to carry out operations on different data without having to be aware of how those operations are implemented. Suppose, for example, you want to find the product of two numbers, either of which may be of type **int** or **double**. You declare and define four functions, all with the same name, to ensure a correct result regardless of the types of the arguments used in a call to the function.

```
// Overloaded function prototypes

int prod_func(int, int);
double prod_func(int, double);
double prod_func(double, int);
double prod_func(double, double);
```

The full text of the functions is not shown; we assume that the types and arithmetic operations are properly handled by them. In C, you'd have to define four functions with different names. The C++ compiler chooses the appropriate function instance depending on the syntax of the function call that you write:

```
double prod;
    ...
prod = prod_func(15, 2.718281828);
```

This code causes the function declared by the second prototype to be called.

Example: overloaded functions

Here's a program that uses overloaded functions to find the squares of numbers.

Squares

```
#include  <iostream.h>

float   sqr_func(float);
doublesqr_func(double);
doublesqr_func(float,  float);

int  main()
{
    float  f = 1.7320508;
    double  d = 2.236068;

    cout << "Square of " << f << " is: " << sqr_func(f) << "\n";
    cout << "Square of " << d << " is: " << sqr_func(d) << "\n";
    cout << f << " multiplied by itself is "<< sqr_func(f, f) << "\n";
    return(0);
}

float sqr_func(float  f)
{
    return(f * f);
}

double  sqr_func(double  d)
{
    return(d * d);
}

double  sqr_func(float f1, float f2)
{
    return(f1  * f2);
}
```

> Function 'sqr_func' overloaded

The results output by this program are:

```
Square of 1.732051 is: 3
Square of 2.236068 is: 5
1.732051 multiplied by itself is 3
```

There are three instances of **sqr_func**, all with different argument lists. The compiler selects the appropriate function depending on the arguments used in the function call. The criteria the compiler uses to make the selection are explained in the next section. Some basic selection rules follow.

- The compiler does not use the return type of the function to distinguish between function instances.

- The argument lists of each of the function instances must be different.

- Whether or not argument names supplied in a function call match the corresponding parameter names in the function definition does not affect the selection process.

Use of prototypes such as these, with matching function definitions later in the code, results in compilation errors:

```
float  sqr_func(float);
double  sqr_func(float);
```

The compiler interprets the function **sqr_func** as having been defined identically twice, regardless of the different return types.

Example: overloaded class member functions

You can use overloaded functions in defining classes, as well as in the procedural way, shown in the previous example. Here's a class implementation of the squares program.

The program uses a simple class, **number**, which defines one private integer member. This variable, **num**, is initialised by a simple constructor and its value retrieved in the function code using an access function. The value of **num** is assigned to the local variable **i**. The different instances of the overloaded function **sqr_func** are called depending on the type of **i** in the function calls.

Squares with class

```cpp
#include  <iostream.h>

class  number
{
private:
    int num;
public:
    number() { num = 5; }  // constructor
    int Num() { return(num); }      // access function

    int sqr_func(int);
    float sqr_func(float);
    double  sqr_func(double);
};

int main()
{
    number n;
    int i = n.Num();

    cout << n.sqr_func(i) << "\n";
    cout << n.sqr_func( float(i) ) << "\n";
    cout << n.sqr_func( (double)i ) << "\n";
    return(0);
}

int number::sqr_func(int i)
{
    cout << "Returning int square: ";
    return(i * i);
}

float number::sqr_func(float f)
{
    cout << "Returning float square: ";
    return(f * f);
}

double number::sqr_func(double d)
{
    cout << "Returning double square: ";
    return(d * d);
}
```

> Function 'sqr_func' overloaded

> The C (also C++) typecast notation is used in the **double** call; the C++ equivalent is used for the **float** call. Either way, the typecast converts the integer **i** to float or double.

The results output by the program are:

```
Returning int square: 25
Returning float square: 25
Returning double square: 25
```

Function call resolution

When you call an overloaded function, there are three possible results:

● A single function instance is matched by the compiler to the function call and this instance is called.

● Multiple, ambiguous, matches are found by the compiler, which is unable to select between them. A compilation error results.

● No match can be found by the compiler and an error results.

This program illustrates all three cases.

```c
#include    <iostream.h>

float  sqr_func(float);
double   sqr_func(double);

int  main()
{
    float   f = 1.7320508;
    double  d = 2.236068;
    int    i = 5;
    int     *ip = &i;

    cout << "Square of " << f << " is: " << sqr_func(f) << "\n";
    cout << "Square of " << d << " is: " << sqr_func(d) << "\n";
    cout << "Square of " << i << " is: " << sqr_func(i) << "\n";
    cout << "Square of " << ip << " is: " << sqr_func(ip) << "\n";
    return(0);
}
```

```
float sqr_func(float f)
{
    return(f * f);
}

double sqr_func(double d)
{
    return(d * d);
}
```

The calls to the function **sqr_func** using **double** and **float** arguments are successfully matched.

The call using the integer argument is matched by promotion of the integer to either **float** or **double** type but is ambiguous and causes a compilation error: the compiler does not know which function instance to call as either promotion is equally valid.

There is no matching function declaration or definition for the call using the pointer argument. This causes a compilation error.

Take note

When using overloaded functions, you should ensure that the order and type of arguments in the call match the argument list in one (and only one) instance of the overloaded function. If the match is not exact, the C++ compiler will try very hard to resolve the function call to a match, but it is better to avoid this altogether.

Operator overloading

Operator overloading is a special case of function overloading. You are allowed to assign additional meanings to most of the C++ *basic operators,* like < (less than) and * (multiply). This means that you can define operators to do special processing not defined as part of C++.

The C++ basic operators that you may overload are:

!	~	+	-	*	&	/	%
< <	> >	<	< =	>	> =	= =	! =
^	|	& &	>	+ =	- =	* =	/ =
% =	& =	^ =	|=	< < =	> > =	,	-> *
->	()	[]	=	+ +	—	n e w	delete

The operators on the last row have some special characteristics when overloaded (which can be regarded as advanced overloading; see the *Newnes C++ Pocket Book*). For example, if you're a masochist, you can dispense with the memory-management provided by your operating system and do it yourself, by overloading the **new** operator. This book confines itself to non-advanced overloading and overloading the assignment, which is needed to provide a full range of class services.

You aren't allowed overload these operators:

.	.*	::	?:

C++ doesn't allow new operators to be introduced by this means. If you want to overload an operator, you must take it from the set of overloadable operators. For example, you might want to use := to denote assignment, as in Pascal, and to overload the equality operator == with the C++ assignment operator =. The introduction of := is illegal; the overloading of == with = is legal but confusing and undesirable.

To overload an operator, create a function named by the keyword **operator** immediately followed by the actual text of the operator to be overloaded. In this example, we overload the addition operator, +.

```
char  add_char::operator+(add_char&  c2)
{
    // operator function code
}
```

This definition means that the overloaded-operator function named by **operator+**, which has a single class-object parameter **c2**, carries out on **c2** and the class of which **operator+** is a member (**add_char**) a set of operations specified by the code in the body of the function.

The function name **operator+** need not be a contiguous string. Any number of spaces may surround the operator symbol +.

Example: overloading addition

This example program, called **add_char.cpp**, uses the class **add_char** and a member function which is the addition operator overloaded.

The purpose of the program is to perform alphabetic addition of characters using a + operator overloaded to do that special kind of addition. In the convention used by the program, **c** added to **a** is **d**; and **h** added to **g** is **o**. There is a mixed-type expression in the operator function that does the actual alphabetic addition.

The declaration of class **add_char** contains one private data member, **c**, of type **char**. It has three member functions: a constructor to initialise **c** to an alphabetic value; an access function to retrieve the value of **c**; and an overloaded-operator function giving a new meaning to the operator +.

In the **main** function, we define two instances of **add_char**, **c1** and **c2** and their data members initialised by the constructor to **g** and **h** respectively. We assign a local variable, **sum**, the result of the overloaded-operator function call:

```
c1 + c2
```

The last statement in **main** displays that result:

```
'Sum' of g and h is o
```

Here is its header for the overloaded-operator function **operator+**:

```
char  add_char::operator+(add_char&  c2)
```

This specifies one parameter, a reference to the class object **c2** corresponding to the operand on the right of the overloaded addition **c1 + c2**. Here, the operand **c2** is the argument to the overloaded-operator function **operator+**. The operand used as an argument in the

```
add_char.cpp
```

```cpp
#include   <iostream.h>
class   add_char
{
private:
    char  c;
public:
    add_char(char c_in) { c = c_in; }      // constructor
    char operator+(add_char&  c2);         // overloaded '+'
    char c_pr()                            // access function
    {
        return(c);
    }
};

int  main()
{
    add_char   c1('g');
    add_char   c2('h');
    char  sum;
    sum = c1 + c2;
    cout << "'Sum' of " << c1.c_pr() << " and "
         << c2.c_pr() << " is " << sum << "\n";
    return(0);
}

char  add_char::operator+(add_char&   c2)
{
    return(c + (c2.c - ('a' - 1)));
}
```

> Add to the c1 character the alphabetic displacement of the c2 character. This gives the 'sum' of the two characters.

operator+ function call doesn't have to have the same name as the function parameter. If these class instances are defined and initialised:

```cpp
add_char   x1('c');
add_char   x2('d');
```

it's OK to make **x1** and **x2** operands of the overloaded operator:

```cpp
sum = x1 + x2;
```

The operand **x2** is then copied *through the reference* to the **operator+** parameter **c2**. Use of the reference declaration **add_char& c2** in the case of a simple class like **add_char** is not necessary, although it improves efficiency because copying a reference parameter imposes less overhead than copying a full class instance.

The overloaded-operator function **operator+** is also passed an implicit **this** pointer to **c1**. The function can therefore directly access the data member **c** of **c1**.

In the **return** statement:

```
return(c + (c2.c - ('a' - 1)));
```

c is the private data member of **c1**, accessed using the implicit **this** pointer. Its contents are added arithmetically to those of **c2.c**, offset from the start of the alphabet. This is an ordinary, not an overloaded, addition. You could write it with the **this** pointer explicitly included:

```
return(this->c + (c2.c - ('a' - 1)));
```

Also, you can write the assignment to **sum**:

```
sum = c1.operator+(c2);
```

which may help you understand how the **operator+** function receives an implicit **this** pointer referring to class object **c1**.

If you overload the assignment operator, =, the overloading function must be a member of a class. Functions overloading most other operators do not have to be class members but must take at least one argument that is a class object. This is designed to prevent a C++ basic operator being redefined unreasonably to operate on two non-class data objects. An example of unreasonable use would be to redefine the multiplication operator ***** to mean division when used with integers.

Even with operator overloading, normal precedence and associativity rules apply. Thus, no matter how you might overload + and *****:

```
a + b * c
```

will always be evaluated as:

```
a + (b * c)
```

You can't overload a basic operator that is strictly unary or binary to mean the opposite:

```
!x      //    '!' is always unary
17 % 6  //    '%' is always binary
```

In overloading operators try to mimic the purpose of the equivalent basic operator. The overloading of + in **add_char.cpp** is intuitive; + being overloaded to cause subtraction of characters would not be.

Overloading the assignment: deep and shallow copy

Overloading the assignment operator presents a number of difficult underlying issues and yet you need to know about it. In this section, I give an overview of the mechanism and the side-effects of assignment that it is intended to overcome. The **string** class example (page 87) gives the details of the code to implement the overloaded assignment.

A class instance may be assigned to another of the same type. By default, *memberwise assignment* – a blind *bitwise* copy – is used. If the class objects contain pointer members, memory will become corrupted when those pointers are deallocated. Here's why: suppose we assign class instance **inst1** to **inst2** and that **inst1** has a pointer member **p** that points to some dynamically-allocated memory. Before the copy, the objects can be shown with the diagram:

where the member, **p**, of **inst1** points to an area of memory. After the assignment, this is the situation:

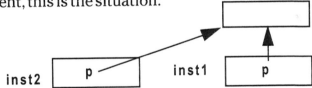

We've done a *shallow copy*, copying the pointers but not the memory they point to. Both now point to the same area of memory. When **inst1** and **inst2** are about to go out of scope, calls to the destructor for them will try (twice) to deallocate the same memory, causing a runtime error. Overloading the assignment operator avoids this double-deallocation.

Suppose we have a class called **ptrclass**, containing a pointer member, **p**. We have two instances of the class, **inst1** and **inst2**. Here's how you'd overload the assignment operator so that memory doesn't get corrupted on assignment of one instance to the other:

```
class ptrclass
{
private:
    char *p;
```

```
public:
    //    public members here
    ptrclass&   operator=(ptrclass&);
    ~ptrclass() { delete p; }
};
```

> Overloaded assignment operator copies memory within instances

The **operator=** function takes as its parameter a reference to the class instance on the right of the overloaded assignment. When called, it is implicitly passed a **this** pointer to the class instance on the left. It modifies that instance and returns a reference to it as the result of the assignment.

```
//  'operator='
ptrclass&  ptrclass::operator=(ptrclass&  inst1)
{
        return(*this);
}
```

> Copy the *memory at* **inst1.ptr** to the *memory at* **inst2.ptr**, *not* the pointer **inst1** to **inst2**.

You do the overloaded assignment of the two instances like this:

```
inst2 = inst1;
```

which can also be written as:

```
inst2.operator=(inst1);
```

The **operator=** function is called with a reference to **inst1** as an argument. We now copy the memory pointed to by **inst1.p** to the memory pointed to by **inst2.p**. (See the copy constructor function of the **string** class example, page 86). By copying the memory at the pointers rather than just the pointers, we perform a *deep copy* and ensure that the pointers don't get corrupted. Memory after the assignment looks like this:

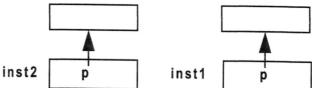

Finally, the statement **return(*this)** returns a reference to the changed contents of **inst2** to the assignment. This way the contents of **inst1** are copied to **inst2** without the unwanted side-effects referred to above.

To prevent further pointer corruption, both the parameter and return value of **operator=** *must be references to the operands of the overloaded assignment.*

Assignment and initialisation

You've seen in the last section that shallow copy, or memberwise assignment, causes memory corruption. So does initialisation when it's done in either of the two ways:

```
ptrclass  inst2(inst1);
ptrclass  inst2  =  inst1;
```

In each case of initialisation such as this, the compiler generates a default copy mechanism (a *default copy constructor*) that does a blind member-by-member initialisation, referred to as *memberwise initialisation*. This is similar to memberwise assignment and messes up memory in the same ways. You can resolve these problems by providing tailored *copy constructors* that perform *smart assignment* of pointers which are class members.

I've shown two cases of class-instance initialisation. There are two others:

● When a function receives a class instance as an argument.

● When a function returns a class instance.

For all four cases, you need a copy constructor to prevent corruption of memory.

Initialising objects with copy constructors

A copy constructor is one that is called to initialise the class instance of which it is a member to the value of another class instance.

In the case of the class **X**, the prototype of the copy constructor looks like this:

```
X::X(const  X&);
```

If no copy constructor is defined for a class, then initialising operations cause the default copy constructor to be called quietly. The default copy constructor isn't very refined, performing as it does simple memberwise initialisation.

To see a case where we need a copy constructor, look at the class **coord**:

```
class coord
{
private:
    int *x_coord, *y_coord;
public:
    coord(int x, int y)
    {
        cout << "Constructing....\n";
        x_coord  = new int;
        *x_coord = x;
        y_coord  = new int;
        *y_coord = y;
    }
    void print()
    {
        cout << *x_coord << " " << *y_coord << "\n";
    }
    ~coord()
    {
        cout << "Destructing....\n";
        delete x_coord;
        delete y_coord;
    }
};
```

Defining an instance of **coord**:

```
coord  point1(5,10);
```

works fine, with memory to accommodate the arguments **5** and **10** being allocated to the pointers **x_coord** and **y_coord** by the constructor function. It's when we try to do either of the initialising operations:

```
coord  point2(point1);
coord point2 = point1;
```

that we run into the shallow-copy memory-corruption problem which I described in the last section.

In both cases, the default copy constructor initialises the pointer values in **point2** with those stored in **point1**. The destructor, which is called twice, then attempts to deallocate the same memory twice. The results of doing this are undefined but are always an error and may cause the program to crash.

The problem is resolved using a specially-written copy constructor, which is added to **coord** as a function member:

```
coord(const coord& copypoint)
{
    cout << "Copy constructing....\n";
    x_coord = new int;
    *x_coord = *(copypoint.x_coord);
    y_coord = new int;
    *y_coord = *(copypoint.y_coord);
}
```

The class **point2** is initialised by an explicit call to the copy constructor. In the earlier example, the default copy constructor shallow-copied the pointer values **x_coord** and **y_coord**, leading to an attempted double memory deallocation. This time the *integer objects pointed to* by **x_coord** and **y_coord** are copied to newly-allocated memory in **point2**. When the destructor is eventually called twice, it each time deallocates different memory.

With the copy constructor included in the **coord** class, initialisation of class instances in any of the four ways described at the start of this section will use the copy constructor and not the default copy constructor. The resulting initialisation is error-free.

Example: a string class

The character string – strictly, the null-terminated character array – is one of the data objects most commonly used in C and C++ programming. A large number of string operations are also defined, including those provided in the standard libraries. The ANSI C++ class library additionally defines a general purpose **string** class.

Because it illustrates well so many aspects of class implementation and class services in C++, this section presents a **string** class example, in no way intended as an alternative to the standard string class. First, the **string** class is declared as part of the header file **str.h**:

str.h (header)

```
class string
{
private:
    char *sptr;
    int   slen;
    int   ssize;
public:
    string();
    string(int);
    string(const char *);
    string(const string &);
    void set_str(const char *);
    char *access() { return(sptr); }

    void  operator+=(string&);

    string&  operator=(string&);

    ~string() { delete sptr; }
};

extern const int MAX;
```

Copy constructor

Binary operator-overload function for string concatenation

Overloaded assignment operator, copies strings

The class **string** defines a character pointer **sptr** as a private data member, along with length and array-size information. The four constructor functions in different ways allocate space for this pointer and initialise the resulting character array as a string. The fourth constructor in the list is the copy constructor for the **string** class. The destructor deallocates memory reserved for string instances. The two overloaded operator functions implement string concatenation and assignment.

The class defines an access function – called **access** – to retrieve the value of **sptr**. and the function **set_str** to set the text value of a **string** instance. The code implementing the four constructors and the other member functions is in the program file **strfunc.cpp**:

strfunc.cpp (functions)

```
#include   <iostream.h>
#include   <string.h>
#include   "str.h"

string::string()                          String  constructors
{
    sptr = new char[MAX];
    ssize = MAX;
    *sptr = '\0';
    slen = 0;
}
string::string(int  size)
{
    sptr = new char[size];
    ssize = size;
    *sptr = '\0';
    slen = 0;
}
string::string(const  char  *s_in)
{
    slen = ssize = strlen(s_in) + 1;
    sptr = new char[slen];
    strcpy(sptr,  s_in);
                                          Copy  constructor
}

string::string(const  string&  ob_in)
{
    slen = ssize = strlen(ob_in.sptr) + 1;
    sptr = new char[slen];
    strcpy(sptr,  ob_in.sptr);
}
```

```
    void string::set_str(const char *s_in)
    {
        delete sptr;
        slen = ssize = strlen(s_in) + 1;
        sptr = new char[slen];
        strcpy(sptr, s_in);
    }
    void string::operator+=(string& s2)
    {
        char *ap;
        slen += (s2.slen + 1);
        ap = new char[slen];
        strcpy(ap, sptr);
        strcat(ap, s2.sptr);
        delete sptr;
        ssize = slen;
        sptr = new char[slen];
        strcpy(sptr, ap);
    }
    string& string::operator=(string& s2)
    {
        if (this == &s2)
            return(*this);

        delete sptr;
        sptr = new char[s2.slen];

        slen = ssize = s2.slen;
        strcpy(sptr, s2.sptr);

        return(*this);
    }
```

'operator=' -- assigns strings

Watch for the case of assignment of the same class! (e.g: s1 = s1 would mean losing the string)

Deallocate string space in class object (this) being copied to, then re-allocate enough space for the object being copied

Copy the string and its length

Return this class object to the assignment

The first constructor allocates to the pointer **sptr** a character array of fixed length **MAX**. The second allocates an array of length specified by its parameter. The third allocates an array long enough to accommodate the text of its parameter. All three constructors null-terminate the array and set its length counter.

The fourth constructor is the copy constructor. This first finds the length of the text in the incoming **string** instance. It then allocates enough memory to the pointer in the instance being initialised to accommodate that text. Finally, the text (not the pointers!) is copied.

The overloaded functions **operator**+= and **operator**= similarly copy text contents of string instances when such instances are assigned (not initialised!) in the **main** function. The **main** function calls all the functions, as well as (quietly) the destructor, to deallocate memory assigned by the constructors to **sptr**. The code that calls the member functions of **string** is in the **main** function in the program file **str.cpp**:

str.cpp (program)

```
#include  <iostream.h>
#include  "str.h"

const int  MAX = 256;

int  main()
{
    string  s1;
    string  s2(MAX);
    string  s3("and into Mary's bread and jam ");
    string  s4("his sooty foot he put");
    s1.set_str("Mary had a little lamb ");
    s2.set_str("whose feet were black as soot ");
    s1 += s2;                    // overloaded '+='
    s1 += s3;
    s1 += s4;
    string  s5;
    s5 = s1;                     // overloaded  assignment
    cout << "s5: " << s5.access() << endl;
    string  s6(s5);              // copy constructor
    cout << "s6: " << s6.access() << endl;
    string  s7 = s6;             // copy constructor
    cout << "s7: " << s7.access() << endl;
    return(0);
}
```

In essence, the program initialises the string instances **s1**, **s2**, **s3** and **s4** and, with these, sets up **s5**, **s6** and **s7** using the various constructor and overloaded-operator facilities implemented by the class. When the program is run, the nursery rhyme is each time displayed in full by sending to the output stream the contents of the string objects **s5** to **s7**.

Exercises

1. Enumerate, with very short examples, the four cases of initialisation which require a copy constructor.

2. Explain how the chained assignment operation

   ```
   s3 = s2 = s1;
   ```

   is implemented, where **s1**, **s2** and **s3** are objects of the **string** class.

3. Write a program that overloads the stream insertion operator **<<** such that the operand to its right can be a class instance.

4 Classes and inheritance

Introduction

Class inheritance, with virtual functions, is what C++ is all about. Everything you've learnt up to now in this book is essentially groundwork that you have to cover to be able to take advantage of the programming power offered by classes, containing virtual functions, organised in hierarchies.

Classes often have much in common with other classes. Where classes are similar, it's better to define them in terms of common characteristics, instead of duplicating them. With class derivation, C++ allows classes to reuse declarations made in other classes. Derived classes inherit the declarations made in existing base classes.

Let's look at an intuitive example of this process, with the **employee** class example. All employees share certain characteristics: they have a name, date of birth, employee number and grade; all employees are also hired, paid and (maybe) fired.

For specific employee types, we need other data and behaviour. A Manager probably has a salary and bonus, rather than the hourly pay of an ordinary employee. A Supervisor may have a union number. A Line Manager may share some of the characteristics of both the Manager and Supervisor. For example, they may both be entitled to use secretarial services. A director, on the other hand, may have exclusive access to a Personal Assistant. If our company is well off (maybe more likely if it's not!), a Director's perks could include a company-paid yacht in the Caribbean or Mediterranean.

In the employee example, it makes sense to define a generic class called **employee**, holding basic information on the characteristics and behaviour of all employees. Class definitions for **supervisor**, **manager** and the others may then be derived from the **employee** class.

If you use this sort of model with C++, you can get impressive code reuse and serious savings in software development cost compared with more traditional languages such as C. In the diagram, the Technician, Supervisor and Manager classes are derived with single inheritance from Employee. LineManager multiply inherits the characteristics of Supervisor and Manager. You can design and build these class hierarchies as deep as you like.

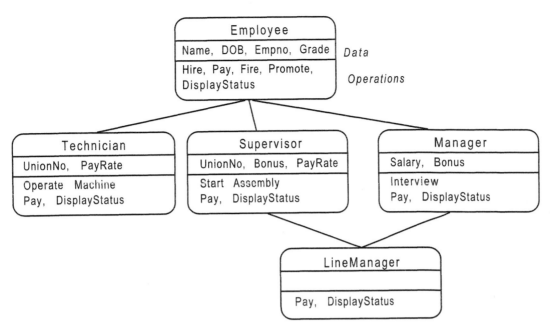

You derive the Supervisor and Manager classes from Employee because they have a lot in common. There are, however, differences of detail in the ways in which similar operations are carried out. For example, all the employees are paid but on different terms and schedules. Displaying the status and qualifications of a director will differ in detail from the equivalent operation for a caretaker.

To deal elegantly with implementing these differences, C++ implements **polymorphism** – the ability to define many different operations that use the same name and present the same interface to the programmer. C++ implements polymorphism using virtual functions declared in a base class and inherited by one or more derived classes. You can use the same function call to carry out a similar (but different) operation for any of the classes in the hierarchy. You have to define different instances of the function for each operation. When the program runs, the runtime system selects the appropriate instance depending on the class instance used in the function call.

With virtual functions, you get a further level of abstraction: the detailed implementations of the different virtual-function instances are hidden and *you don't have to know* what sort of instance (Employee, Manager and so on) you're dealing with in order to, say, pay that employee. With virtual functions, type-checking is reduced and with it the incidence of programmer error.

Class inheritance

Here's the **employee** class hierarchy. We have declarations of the **employee** base class and of three derived classes, **technician**, **supervisor** and **manager**. Don't worry about their full contents yet.

```
class  employee
{
    // no private members, but could be
protected:
    // members hidden from rest of world
public:
    int grade;
    // public class members
};

class technician : public employee
{
private:
    // class members specific to 'technician'
public:
    int unionNo;
    // public member functions can access private members
    // of this class as well as protected members of 'employee'
};

class supervisor : public employee
{
private:
    //
public:
    //
};

class manager : public employee
{
private:
    //
public:
    //
};
```

After the base **employee** class is declared, the declaration:

```
class supervisor : public employee
{
//
};
```

announces a new type, **supervisor**, which inherits all non-private characteristics of **employee** and, between the curly braces, adds zero or more declarations of its own. You must specify the **class** keyword, as well as the names of the two class types, separated by a colon.

The access specifier **public** is optional but usually necessary. When a class is derived from one or more other classes, and when the access specifier **public** is used in the derived class declaration, public members of the base class become public members of the derived class. If **public** is not specified in this way, the members of the derived class are by default private.

Each of **technician**, **supervisor** and **manager** is declared as a derived class of the base class **employee**. Using an object of any of the derived types, you can access all non-private members of the inherited **employee** object as if those members were also members of the derived classes. Here's the code:

```
//  define 'technician' and 'employee' class objects

employee e1;
technician t1;

//  illustrate basic access rules, assuming
//  'public' access specifier in derived-class declarations

e1.grade = 1;    // OK,  grade  is 'employee' member

t1.grade = 1;    // OK,  grade  is 'technician' member
                 // derived from 'employee'

t1.unionNo = 53; // OK,  unionNo  is 'technician' member
                 // not derived from 'employee'

e1.unionNo = 7;  // Error,  unionNo  is not in scope
                 // for 'employee' object
```

This shows that a derived class inherits all non-private members of a base class and that those members are in scope for the derived class. The converse is not true: new members declared in a derived class are not in scope for the base class.

Example: a simple employee class hierarchy

Here's a full-program example, based on the **employee** model, that illustrates single class inheritance and the C++ syntax used to access the members of the classes in a hierarchy.

The program is organised in three program files. **employee.h** contains the class declarations. The program file **empfunc.cpp** defines the member functions of the class hierarchy and **emp.cpp** the small amount of code needed to define class objects and use their members.

employee.h (header)

```cpp
enum qualification {NONE, CERT, DIPLOMA, DEGREE, POSTGRAD};

class employee
{
protected:
    char *name;
    char *dateOfBirth;
    int individualEmployeeNo;
    static int employeeNo;
    int grade;
    qualification employeeQual;
    float accumPay;
public:
    employee();         // constructor
    ~employee();        // destructor
    void pay();
    void promote(int);          // scale increment
    void displayStatus();
};

class technician : public employee
{
private:
    float hourlyRate;
    int unionNo;
public:
    technician();       // constructor
    ~technician();      // destructor
    void pay();
```

The base class **employee**, uniquely, contains a declaration for the function **promote**. The **employee** instance of this function is called no matter which object type – **employee**, **technician**, **supervisor** or **manager** – is used to qualify the promote call.

96

```
      void  displayStatus();
};

class supervisor : public employee
{
private:
    float  monthlyPay;
public:
    supervisor();      // constructor
    ~supervisor();     // destructor
    void  pay();
    void  displayStatus();
};

class manager : public employee
{
private:
    float  monthlyPay;
    float  bonus;
public:
    manager();        // constructor
    ~manager();  // destructor
    void  pay();
    void  displayStatus();
};
```

The classes **technician**, **supervisor** and **manager** are derived from the base class **employee**. All non-private members of **employee** are inherited by and are common to the derived classes.

All the classes have a constructor and a destructor. The constructors do not yet take parameters. Each class defines its own **pay** and **displayStatus** functions. The existence of multiple definitions of these functions does not cause ambiguity. Any call to, say, the **pay** function for a class must, in client code, be qualified with a class instance:

```
//    illustrate 'pay' function call
supervisor    s1;
    ...
s1.pay();     //   not ambiguous
```

You can call the function **pay** without the 's1.' prefix from within a member function of **technician**. In that case, the **pay** function that is a member of **technician** is called.

The program file **empfunc.cpp** contains the code that implements the member functions of the four classes.

empfunc.cpp (functions)

```cpp
#include  <iostream.h>
#include  <string.h>                          string library header
#include  "employee.h"

//      define and initialise static member
int  employee::employeeNo = 1000;

employee::employee()                          Define 'employee'
{                                             member functions first
    char  nameIn[50];

    cout << "Enter new employee name ";
    cin >> nameIn;
    name = new char[strlen(nameIn) + 1];
    strcpy(name,  nameIn);                    C string library function
    dateOfBirth = NULL;
    individualEmployeeNo =  employeeNo++;
    grade = 1;
    employeeQual = NONE;
    accumPay = 0.0;
}
employee::~employee()
{
    delete  name;
    delete  dateOfBirth;
}
void  employee::pay()
{                                             See page 100 for
}                                             use of empty {}
void  employee::promote(int  increment)
{
    grade += increment;
}

void  employee::displayStatus()
{
}
```

```
technician::technician()
{
    hourlyRate = 5.4;
    unionNo    = 0;
    cout << "Hourly employee " << name << " is hired" << endl;
}
technician::~technician()
{
    cout << "Hourly employee " << name << " is fired!" << endl;
}
void  technician::pay()
{
    float paycheck;
    paycheck = hourlyRate * 40;
    accumPay += paycheck;
    cout << "Hourly employee " << individualEmployeeNo
        << " paid " << paycheck << endl;
}
void   technician::displayStatus()
{
    cout << "Hourly employee " << individualEmployeeNo
        << " is of grade " << grade << " and has been paid "
        << accumPay << " so far this year" << endl;
}


supervisor::supervisor()
{
    monthlyPay = 1700.00;
    cout << "Supervisor " << name << " is hired" << endl;
}
supervisor::~supervisor()
{
    cout << "Supervisor " << name << " is fired!" << endl;
}
void  supervisor::pay()
{
    accumPay += monthlyPay;
    cout << "Supervisor " << individualEmployeeNo
        << " paid " << monthlyPay << endl;
}
```

Define 'technician' member functions

Define 'supervisor' member functions

```
void  supervisor::displayStatus()
{
    cout << "Supervisor " << individualEmployeeNo
        << " is of grade " << grade << " and has been paid "
        << accumPay << " so far this year" << endl;
}


manager::manager()
{
    monthlyPay = 2100.00;
    bonus     = 210.0;
    cout << "Manager " << name << " is hired" << endl;
}
manager::~manager()
{
    cout << "Manager " << name << " is fired!" << endl;
}
void  manager::pay()
{
    accumPay += monthlyPay;
    cout << "Manager " << individualEmployeeNo
        << " paid " << monthlyPay << endl;
}
void  manager::displayStatus()
{
    cout << "Manager " << individualEmployeeNo
        << " is of grade " << grade << " and has been paid "
        << accumPay << " so far this year" << endl;
}
```

> Define 'manager' member functions

None of the constructor functions takes any parameters, so the **employee** constructor must prompt the user for input of employee names. In the typical case, no instances of the base class, **employee**, will be created. Two of its member functions, **pay** and **displayStatus**, therefore have no purpose and are empty.

Here's the **main** function. Three class objects are defined, one each for **technician**, **supervisor** and **manager**. In each case, an underlying **employee** object is implicitly defined also.

emp.cpp (program)

```cpp
#include    <iostream.h>
#include    "employee.h"

int  main()
{
    technician  t1;
    supervisor  s1;
    manager     m1;

    t1.pay();
    t1.displayStatus();

    s1.pay();
    s1.displayStatus();

    m1.pay();
    m1.displayStatus();

    return(0);
}
```

The program produces the following output. Text in bold type is what you enter.

Enter new employee name **john**
Hourly employee john is hired
Enter new employee name **chris**
Supervisor chris is hired
Enter new employee name **marilyn**
Manager marilyn is hired
Hourly employee 1000 paid 216
Hourly employee 1000 is of grade 1 and has been paid 216 so far this year
Supervisor 1001 paid 1700
Supervisor 1001 is of grade 1 and has been paid 1700 so far this year
Manager 1002 paid 2100
Manager 1002 is of grade 1 and has been paid 2100 so far this year
Manager marilyn is fired!
Supervisor chris is fired!
Hourly employee john is fired!

User inputs are in **bold**.

Access control

I've already explained the effect of the access-specifier keywords **private** and **public**. Now we also look at the **protected** keyword, as well as the levels of access to members of derived classes that are allowed by various combinations of **private**, **protected** and **public**.

Base class access

Base class access for a derived class is defined by use of any of the access-specifiers **private**, **protected** or **public**.

- In **public** derivation:
  ```
  class manager : public employee
  ```
  manager inherits **protected** and **public** members of **employee** and retains those access levels.

- In **protected** derivation:
  ```
  class manager : protected employee
  ```
  manager inherits **protected** and **public** members of **employee**, but forces all the inherited public members to be protected: you can't access them from client code using an **employee** object.

- In **private** derivation:
  ```
  class manager : private employee
  ```
  all non-private members of **employee** are inherited by **manager** but are now private members of **manager**, regardless of whether they are specified with protected or public access in **employee**.

Public derivation is the default for structures and unions; class derivation defaults to **private**. Here's an example that illustrates many of the possibilities of base class access:

```
class a
{
protected:
    int x;
public:
    int y;
    int z;
};
```

```
class b : private a        // members of a
                           // private in b
{
protected:
    a::x;     // x converted to protected
public:
    a::y;     // y converted to public

    void  myfunc()
    {
        x = 5; // OK, protected
    }
};

int  main()
{
    b  b_inst;

    b_inst.y = 6;  //    OK, public
    b_inst.z = 7;  //    Error, still private
    return(0);
}
```

Class **a** has three data members. Class **b** inherits class **a**, but with
private base class access. Unless their access levels are specifically
converted, **b::x**, **b::y** and **b::z** are private members of class **b** only
accessible by member functions of **b**.

Two explicit conversions are done: **a::x** is converted to a **protected**
member and **a::y** to a **public** member of **b**. **a::z** remains a **private**
member of **b**. Conversions such as these can only reinstate the access
level of a derived member to exactly that specified in the base class
in which it was defined. In the example, **a::x** can only be converted in
class **b** to **protected**, not to **private** or **public**.

After the conversions, **a::x** can be accessed by the function **b::myfunc()**.
Because **a::x** is **protected**, it cannot be directly accessed in **main**. On
the other hand, **a::y** has been reinstated to **public** and is the subject
of an assignment in **main**. Any access to **a::z** using the class variable
b_inst causes a compilation error.

Class member access

- A class member declared with **public** access is visible to all code wherever that class is in scope.

- A class member declared with **private** access is visible wherever that class is in scope, but only to member functions of the class.

- A class member declared with **protected** access is visible wherever that class is in scope, but only to member functions of the class and to member functions of classes derived from it.

Structure members are by default **public**; those of classes are by default **private**. Either may have members that are **protected**. Declaring members protected is only useful if the structure or class in which the declaration is made is to serve as a base class from which others will be derived.

Constructors and destructors

This section considers the order in which constructor and destructor members of a class hierarchy are called and the means by which arguments are passed to constructors in the hierarchy. In a class hierarchy formed of a base class and zero or more derived classes, constructor functions are executed starting with the base class in order of class derivation. Destructor functions are called in reverse order of derivation.

Constructor and destructor functions are never inherited. Therefore, in a class hierarchy, the constructor of a derived class does not take on any of the characteristics of the constructor (if any) declared in its base class.

If a base class constructor takes parameters, you can do the initialisation using the syntax you learnt in Chapter 3. Here's the **employee** base class reworked to declare constructor and destructor functions taking parameters:

```
class  employee
{
protected:
    char  *name;
    char  *dateOfBirth;
    int  individualEmployeeNo;
    static int  employeeNo;
    int grade;
    qualification  employeeQual;
    float  accumPay;
public:
    // constructor: name and grade
    employee(char  *,  int);

    // constructor: name, birthdate, grade, qualification
    employee(char  *,  char  *,  int,  qualification);

    // destructor
    ~employee();

    void  pay();
    void  promote(int);  // scale increment
    void  displayStatus();
};
```

You initialise class instances of type **employee** with definitions like this:

```
employee e1("Karen", 4);
employee e2("John", "580525", 4, DEGREE);
```

The first definition creates a class object **e1** of type **employee** and calls the matching constructor function (the one declaring two parameters in its argument list) to initialise the object with the arguments "**Karen**" and **4**.

In a class hierarchy, what what we usually want is to initialise a derived class instance using a constructor of that derived class. When you create a derived class instance, you also (quietly) make a base class instance. We need a mechanism to call the derived constructor with arguments and then to transmit some, all or none of those arguments to the base class constructor so that the base member variables may be initialised.

Let's look at creation of a derived-class instance of type **technician**. The constructors of both the **employee** and **technician** classes take parameters. The **technician** class declaration is this:

```
class technician : public employee
{
private:
    float   hourlyRate;
    int     unionNo;
public:
    // name, grade, rate, union ID
    technician(char *, int, float, int);

    // name, birthdate, grade, qualification, rate, union ID
    technician(char *, char *, int, qualification, float, int);

    // destructor
    ~technician();

    void  pay();
    void  displayStatus();
};
```

You write the header of the second constructor function of the **technician** class like this:

```
technician::technician(char    *nameIn,
                char *birthIn,
                int  gradeIn,
                  qualification qualIn,
                float rateIn,
                int  unionNoIn)
            : employee(nameIn, birthIn, gradeIn, qualIn)
```

Four of the six parameters received by the **technician** constructor arguments are passed on to the matching **employee** constructor. The **technician** constructor takes its own parameters, **rateIn** and **unionNoIn**, and assigns them to the member variables **hourlyRate** and **unionNo** of its class.

Example: class hierarchy with constructors taking parameters

employee.h (header)

```
enum    qualification    {NONE,CERT,DIPLOMA,DEGREE,POSTGRAD};

class  employee
{
protected:
    char  *name;
    char  *dateOfBirth;
    int   individualEmployeeNo;
    static int employeeNo;
    int  grade;
    qualification   employeeQual;
    float  accumPay;
public:
    // constructor: name and grade
    employee(char  *,  int);

    // constructor: name, birthdate, grade, qualification
    employee(char  *,  char  *,  int,  qualification);
```

```cpp
        ~employee(); // destructor

    void pay();
    void promote(int); // scale increment
    void displayStatus();
};

class technician : public employee
{
private:
    float hourlyRate;
    int    unionNo;
public:
    // name, grade, rate, union ID
    technician(char *, int, float, int);

    // name, birthdate, grade, qualification, rate, union ID
    technician(char *, char *, int, qualification, float, int);

    ~technician();// destructor

    void pay();
    void displayStatus();
};

class supervisor : public employee
{
private:
    float  monthlyPay;
public:
    // name, grade, rate
    supervisor(char *, int, float);

    // name, birthdate, grade, qualification, rate
    supervisor(char *, char *, int, qualification, float);

    ~supervisor();// destructor

    void pay();
    void displayStatus();
};
```

```
class manager : public employee
{
private:
    float  monthlyPay;
    float  bonus;
public:
    // name, grade, rate, bonus
    manager(char *, int, float, float);

    // name, birthdate, grade, qualification, rate, bonus
    manager(char *, char *, int, qualification, float, float);

    ~manager(); // destructor

    void  pay();
    void  displayStatus();
};
```

We implement the member functions of all four classes in the program file **empfunc.cpp**:

empfunc.cpp (functions)

```
#include  <iostream.h>
#include  <string.h>
#include  "employee.h"

// define and initialise static member
int  employee::employeeNo = 1000;

employee::employee(char *nameIn, int gradeIn)
{
    name = new char[strlen(nameIn) + 1];
    strcpy(name,  nameIn);
    dateOfBirth = NULL;
    individualEmployeeNo = employeeNo++;
    grade = gradeIn;
    employeeQual = NONE;
    accumPay = 0.0;
}
```

Define 'employee' member functions first

```
employee::employee(char    *nameln,
          char *birthln,
          int gradeln,
          qualification qualln)
{
    name = new char[strlen(nameln) + 1];
    strcpy(name,  nameln);
    dateOfBirth = new char[strlen(birthln) + 1];
    strcpy(dateOfBirth,  birthln);
    grade = gradeln;
    employeeQual = qualln;
    individualEmployeeNo  =  employeeNo++;
    accumPay = 0.0;
}
employee::~employee()
{
    delete  name;
    delete  dateOfBirth;
}
void  employee::pay()
{
}
void  employee::promote(int  increment)
{
    grade += increment;
}
void  employee::displayStatus()
{
}
technician::technician(char   *nameln,
          int  gradeln,
          float rateln,
          int  unionNoln)
           : employee(nameln, gradeln)
{
    hourlyRate = rateln;
    unionNo     = unionNoln;
    cout << "Hourly employee " << name << " is hired" << endl;
}
technician::technician(char   *nameln,
          char *birthln,
          int  gradeln,
```

Define 'technician'
member functions

```
                    qualification qualIn,
                    float rateIn,
                    int   unionNoIn)
                      : employee(nameIn, birthIn, gradeIn, qualIn)
{
    hourlyRate = rateIn;
    unionNo    = unionNoIn;
    cout << "Hourly employee " << name << " is hired" << endl;
}
technician::~technician()
{
    cout << "Hourly employee " << name << " is fired!" << endl;
}
void  technician::pay()
{
    float paycheck;
    paycheck = hourlyRate * 40;
    accumPay += paycheck;
    cout << "Hourly employee " << individualEmployeeNo
         << " paid " << paycheck << endl;
}
void  technician::displayStatus()
{
    cout << "Hourly employee " << individualEmployeeNo
         << " is of grade " << grade << " and has been paid "
         << accumPay << " so far this year" << endl;
}

supervisor::supervisor(char   *nameIn,
              int   gradeIn,
              float rateIn)
                : employee(nameIn, gradeIn)
{
    monthlyPay = rateIn;
    cout << "Supervisor " << name << " is hired" << endl;
}
supervisor::supervisor(char   *nameIn,
              char *birthIn,
              int   gradeIn,
              qualification qualIn,
              float rateIn)
                : employee(nameIn, birthIn, gradeIn, qualIn)
```

Define 'supervisor' member functions
```

```

```
{
    monthlyPay = rateIn;
    cout << "Supervisor " << name << " is hired" << endl;
}
supervisor::~supervisor()
{
    cout << "Supervisor " << name << " is fired!" << endl;
}
void supervisor::pay()
{
    accumPay += monthlyPay;
    cout << "Supervisor " << individualEmployeeNo
        << " paid " << monthlyPay << endl;
}
void supervisor::displayStatus()
{
    cout << "Supervisor " << individualEmployeeNo
        << " is of grade " << grade << " and has been paid "
        << accumPay << " so far this year" << endl;
}
manager::manager(char   *nameIn,
        int  gradeIn,
        float rateIn,
        float bonusIn)
            : employee(nameIn, gradeIn)
{
    monthlyPay = rateIn;
    bonus      = bonusIn;
    cout << "Manager " << name << " is hired" << endl;
}
manager::manager(char   *nameIn,
        char *birthIn,
        int  gradeIn,
        qualification qualIn,
        float rateIn,
        float bonusIn)
            : employee(nameIn, birthIn, gradeIn, qualIn)
{
    monthlyPay = rateIn;
    bonus      = bonusIn;
    cout << "Manager " << name << " is hired" << endl;
}
```

Define 'manager'
member functions

```
manager::~manager()
{
    cout << "Manager " << name << " is fired!" << endl;
}
void  manager::pay()
{
    accumPay  += monthlyPay;
    cout << "Manager " << individualEmployeeNo
         << " paid " << monthlyPay << endl;
}
void  manager::displayStatus()
{
    cout << "Manager " << individualEmployeeNo
         << " is of grade " << grade << " and has been paid "
         << accumPay << " so far this year" << endl;
}
```

The **main** function drives the classes and their member functions:

emp.cpp (program)

```
#include  <iostream.h>
#include  "employee.h"

int  main()
{
    technician t1("Mary", 1, 5.40, 1234);
    technician t2("Jane", "651029", 2, CERT, 5.40, 1235);
    supervisor s1("Karen", 4, 1350.00);
    supervisor s2("John", "580525", 4, DEGREE, 1700.00);
    manager m1("Susan", 6, 1350.00, 150.00);
    manager m2
    ("Martin", "580925", 5, POSTGRAD, 1700.00, 200.00);

    t1.pay();
    t1.displayStatus();

    t2.pay();
    t2.displayStatus();
```

```
        s1.pay();
        s1.displayStatus();

        s2.pay();
        s2.displayStatus();

        m1.pay();
        m1.displayStatus();

        m2.pay();
        m2.displayStatus();

        return(0);
    }
```

When you run the program, the output is this:

```
Hourly employee Mary is hired
Hourly employee Jane is hired
Supervisor Karen is hired
Supervisor John is hired
Manager Susan is hired
Manager Martin is hired
Hourly employee 1000 paid 216
Hourly employee 1000 is of grade 1 and has been paid 216 so far this year
Hourly employee 1001 paid 216
Hourly employee 1001 is of grade 2 and has been paid 216 so far this year
Supervisor 1002 paid 1350
Supervisor 1002 is of grade 4 and has been paid 1350 so far this year
Supervisor 1003 paid 1700
Supervisor 1003 is of grade 4 and has been paid 1700 so far this year
Manager 1004 paid 1350
Manager 1004 is of grade 6 and has been paid 1350 so far this year
Manager 1005 paid 1700
Manager 1005 is of grade 5 and has been paid 1700 so far this year
Manager Martin is fired!
Manager Susan is fired!
Supervisor John is fired!
Supervisor Karen is fired!
Hourly employee Jane is fired!
Hourly employee Mary is fired!
```

Multiple inheritance

Up to now, we have considered inheritance by derived classes only of single base classes. A derived class can inherit the characteristics of more than one base class. This facility of C++ reflects and accommodates real-world objects that you may want to simulate.

We could apply the technique to the **employee** class by, for example, actually implementing the **lineManager** class. This is derived from both **supervisor** and **manager**, which in turn have the single base class **employee**. However, multiple inheritance raises a number of complexities and difficult issues which are really beyond the scope of this book. So, if you want to know how to propagate constructor parameters within a multiply-inherited hierarchy, or how to resolve the ambiguity (two instantiations of **employee** for one definition of **lineManager**) in this hierarchy:

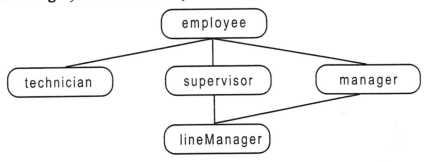

then have a look at the *Newnes C++ Pocket Book*. If you don't want to know this stuff, feel happy about it. Most C++ programs are written with little or no multiple inheritance. There's even a strong body of opinion that multiple inheritance is a Bad Thing and is never necessary. In fact, it's very difficult to contrive a class hierarchy where multiple inheritance is *unavoidable*. So, let's look at the essence of the thing.

Suppose a class **d** is to be declared that inherits the classes **a**, **b** and **c**. Classes **a** and **c** are to be inherited by **d** with public access, and **b** with private access. Here is the syntax for declaration, with multiple inheritance, of class **d**:

```
class d : public a, private b, public c
{
//    'class d' declarations
};
```

The constructor functions of a singly-inherited hierarchy of classes are executed in order of class derivation. The same is true for hierarchies containing classes derived from multiple bases.

If the base classes have constructor functions, the constructors are executed, left to right, in the same order as that in which the base classes are specified. Destructors are invoked in the reverse order. This is a generalisation of the execution-order rules given in the last section, as a simple example shows:

```cpp
#include  <iostream.h>

class  base
{
public:
    base() { cout << "Constructing 'base'\n"; }
    ~base() { cout << "Destructing 'base'\n"; }
};

class  a : public base
{
public:
    a() { cout << "Constructing 'a'\n"; }
    ~a() { cout << "Destructing 'a'\n"; }
};

class  b
{
public:
    b() { cout << "Constructing 'b'\n"; }
    ~b() { cout << "Destructing 'b'\n"; }
};

class  c
{
public:
    c() { cout << "Constructing 'c'\n"; }
    ~c() { cout << "Destructing 'c'\n"; }
};

class  d : public a, public b, public c
{
public:
```

```
        d() { cout << "Constructing 'd'\n"; }
        ~d() { cout << "Destructing 'd'\n"; }
};

int main()
{
        d d1;  // define instance of 'd'
        return(0);
}
```

Here we have a base class **base**, from which **a** is derived. Classes **b** and **c** are separately declared and **a, b** and **c** in turn are base classes of **d**. When an instance, **d1**, of class **d** is defined in the **main** function, the constructors are invoked in the order of derivation and the destructors are executed in reverse order. The order can be traced from the program's output:

```
Constructing  'base'
Constructing  'a'
Constructing  'b'
Constructing  'c'
Constructing  'd'
Destructing  'd'
Destructing  'c'
Destructing  'b'
Destructing  'a'
Destructing  'base'
```

Any or all of the constructor functions in a class hierarchy containing classes derived from multiple bases may require arguments. The order of execution of the constructors and destructors can be described as left-to-right, top-to-bottom. If you define an instance of **lineManager**, the order of constructor calls will be this:

```
employee
supervisor
employee
manager
lineManager
```

Any constructors are transmitted 'up the hierarchy' in a manner which is a logical extension to that you've already seen in the previous section but, for more on this, I refer you to the *C++ Pocket Book*.

Virtual functions

You can use a pointer to a base class object to point to any class derived from that object. This fact is critically important in the use of virtual functions and for the C++ implementation of polymorphism.

If you use a pointer of base class type to call a member function of a class hierarchy, the base class instance of the function is always called. Otherwise, to call a function for a particular class object, the type of that object must be known to the programmer.

Consider the **pay** member functions of the class **employee** and the derived class **manager**. Let's define instances of both and a pointer of base class (**employee**) type:

```
employee  e1;
manager   m1;
employee  *ep
```

If the pointer is set pointing to **e1**:

```
ep = &e1;
```

then the function call:

```
ep->pay();
```

results in a call to **employee::pay()**. If the pointer is set to **m1**:

```
ep = &m1;
```

(which is quite legal), the function call:

```
ep->pay();
```

still results in the function **employee::pay()**, and *not* the **manager** instance of **pay**, being called. In short, to call **manager::pay()**, you'd need a pointer of type **manager**. Maintaining pointers of many different but related types is a nuisance.

It would be useful if this restriction were removed and a base-class pointer such as **e1** could be used to access instances of any derived class in the same hierarchy. Then you could use one pointer to point to objects of different types and allow generic processing to be done on objects of those types.

This is the essence of polymorphism as implemented by C++. Only one small addition to your knowledge of C++ syntax is needed to achieve polymorphism – the function **employee::pay()** must be specified **virtual** in the declaration of the class **employee**. Then you can use the pointer **ep** to access the redefinition of the function that is found in the derived class, rather than always accessing the base class instance of the function.

You can call a function declared **virtual** in the same way as any other class member function:

```
e1.pay();
```

However, if you call the virtual function with a pointer or reference to a class object, the instance of the function called is the instance defined by that class object.

```
ep = &m1;
ep->pay();// call 'manager' copy of virtual 'pay'
```

All redefinitions in derived classes of a virtual function must have argument lists identical to those of the base declaration of the virtual function.

Hierarchy with virtual functions

Here's a **virtual** version of a simplified **employee** hierarchy, with a full program implementing it. In the base class **employee**, the **pay** function is prefixed with the keyword **virtual**:

employee.h (header)

```
enum  qualification  {NONE,  CERT,  DIPLOMA,  DEGREE,  POSTGRAD};
class  employee
{
protected:
    char  *name;
    char  *dateOfBirth;
    int   individualEmployeeNo;
    static  int  employeeNo;
    int  grade;
    qualification   employeeQual;
    float  accumPay;
public:
    employee();      // constructor
    virtual void pay();
};

class  technician : public  employee
{
private:
    float  hourlyRate;
    int    unionNo;
public:
    technician();              // constructor
    void  promote(int);        // scale increment
    void  pay();
};

class  supervisor : public  employee
{
private:
    float  monthlyPay;
public:
    supervisor();              // constructor
    void  pay();
};
```

Virtual function!

120

```
class manager : public employee
{
private:
    float  monthlyPay;
    float  bonus;
public:
    manager();   // constructor
    void  pay();
};
```

The member functions of the classes are implemented in the program
file **empfunc.cpp**:

empfunc.cpp (functions)

```
#include   <iostream.h>
#include   <string.h>
#include   "employee.h"

//      define and initialise static member
int  employee::employeeNo  =  1000;

employee::employee()
{
    char  nameIn[50];
    strcpy(nameIn,  "Base  Employee");
    name = new char[strlen(nameIn) + 1];
    strcpy(name,   nameIn);
    dateOfBirth = NULL;
    individualEmployeeNo  =  employeeNo++;
    grade = 1;
    employeeQual  =  NONE;
    accumPay  =  0.0;
}

void  employee::pay()
{
    cout  <<  "Base-class  employee  paid!"  <<  endl;
}
```

Define 'employee'
member functions first

```
technician::technician()
{
    strcpy(name,  "Technician");
    hourlyRate = 5.4;
    unionNo    = 0;
}
void technician::promote(int increment)
{
    grade += increment;
}
void  technician::pay()
{
    float  paycheck;

    paycheck = hourlyRate * 40;
    accumPay += paycheck;
    cout << "Technician paid!" << endl;
}

supervisor::supervisor()
{
    strcpy(name,  "Supervisor");
    monthlyPay = 1700.00;
}
void  supervisor::pay()
{
    accumPay += monthlyPay;
    cout << "Supervisor paid!" << endl;
}

manager::manager()
{
    strcpy(name,  "Manager");
    monthlyPay = 2100.00;
    bonus      = 210.0;
}

void  manager::pay()
{
    accumPay += monthlyPay;
    cout << "Manager paid!" << endl;
}
```

Define 'technician' member functions

Define 'supervisor' member functions

Define 'manager' member functions

Code in the **main** function is used to exercise the classes:

emp.cpp (program)

```
#include   <iostream.h>
#include   "employee.h"

int  main()
{
    employee e1;
    techniciant1;
    supervisors1;

    employee *ep = &e1;
    technician*tp = &t1;
    supervisor*sp = &s1;

    ep->pay();// call base-class 'pay'

    ep = &t1;
    ep->pay();// call 'technician' 'pay'

    ep = &s1;
    ep->pay();// call 'supervisor' 'pay'
    return(0);
}
```

When you run the program, the results are these:

```
Base-class  employee  paid!
Technician  paid!
Supervisor  paid!
```

After the first line is output, the base class object pointer **eptr** is assigned the address of the **technician** class object **t1**:

```
eptr = &t1;
```

Because **eptr** has been assigned a pointer of type **technician ***, then, when the function call is made:

```
eptr->pay();
```

123

the redefinition of the **pay** function contained in the derived class **technician** is selected at runtime and executed. When **eptr** is assigned the address of the **supervisor** class object **s1**, the function call **eptr->pay();** causes **supervisor::pay()** to be selected at runtime and executed.

A redefinition of a virtual function in a derived class is said to *override*, rather than overload, the base class instance of the function. The difference is important because, unlike in the case of ordinary function overloading, the resolution of virtual function calls is done at runtime. The process is referred to as late, or dynamic, binding.

It's OK for a derived class not to override a virtual function defined in a base class: it contains no redefinition of the virtual function. In such a case, the base class instance of the function is called even if a pointer to the derived class is used in the function call.

Virtual functions are inherited through multiple levels in a derived class hierarchy. If a virtual function is defined only in a base class, that definition is inherited by all the derived classes.

Another difference between virtual functions and overloaded functions is that virtual functions must be class members, while overloaded functions do not have to be.

Abstract classes

As part of the process of designing a class hierarchy, you often have to declare a base class that itself serves no useful purpose. Such a base class is usually the common denominator of more concrete classes derived from it.

The **employee** class is quite a good example of such a class. If you think about it, you've never seen an *employee*. You've seen a *manager*, a *secretary*, a *supervisor* and so on, but never an abstract *employee*. Even the operation of paying the **employee** by calling the function **employee::pay()** does not mean very much – it being more common to pay real rather than generic employees. This is why **employee::pay()** is left empty in the earlier examples of this chapter.

The function **employee::pay()** currently displays the message:

```
Base-class employee paid!
```

Most likely, in a real program, it would do nothing and be defined only to serve as a base virtual function for the **pay** functions in the derived classes, which actually do some processing. Where there is a dummy virtual function like this, a different declaration can be used and the dummy definition discarded:

```
virtual void pay() = 0;
```

Now there is no instance of **employee::pay()** and the declaration is called a *pure virtual function*. The pure virtual function must be overridden by one or more functions in a derived class. Formally, a class that contains at least one pure virtual function is called an *abstract class*.

Exercises

1. In this derived class hierarchy, fill in the constructor functions needed to initialise **i**, **a** and **d** following the creation of an object of type **c**:

    c c_inst(1.732, 'x', 5);

```
class a
{
public:
    int i;
    ...
};
class b : public a
{
public:
    char ch;
    ...
};
class c : public b
{
public:
    double d;
    ...
};
```

2. Given this class hierarchy, add to each class a constructor function. The **employee** constructor should take three parameters; the **manager** constructor should take five. Each constructor should assign values to the data members of its class. Show how the arguments used in the definition of an instance of the class **manager** are distributed between the **manager** and **employee** constructors.

```
class employee
{
protected:
    int grade;
    int employeeNo;
    char name[30];
public:
    void pay();
    void promote();
};
class manager : public employee
{
private:
    double bonus;
    double payRate;
public:
    void payBonus();
};
```

5 ANSI C++ facilities

Function templates

Templates, of which function templates are a special case, are a late addition to C++. The others are *exception handling*, *namespaces* and *run-time type identification* and the four topics are covered in this chapter. All of them also are included in the ANSI C++ Standard.

C++ provides function templates so that you can define a function capable of operating on arguments of any type. You declare a function template by prefixing a function declaration with the **template** keyword followed by a pair of angle-brackets containing one or more identifiers that represent *parameterised types*. This construct is called the *template specification*.

C++ is a strongly typed language. This is mostly a benefit, promoting program reliability, but it causes problems when you need to call a simple function with arguments of types that may vary from call to call. A good example is a function, called **min**, that must find the minimum of two values supplied as arguments. If the function on a first call is to compare two **ints** and on the second two **doubles**, then conventionally you have to make two definitions of the function to handle the two different calls.

Templates provide an elegant solution – here's an example:

```
#include   <iostream.h>

//    template declaration
template<class   num>
num min(num n1, num n2);

int main()
{
    int i1, i2;
    double d1, d2;
    cout << "Enter two integers: ";
    cin >> i1 >> i2;
    cout << "minimum is: " << min(i1, i2) << endl;

    cout << "Enter two doubles: ";
    cin >> d1 >> d2;
    cout << "minimum is: " << min(d1, d2) << endl;
```

Instantiate a **min** template function to compare two *integers*.

Instantiate a **min** template function to compare two *fractions*.

```
    return(0);
}

//    template definition
template<class num>
num min(num n1, num n2)
{
    if (n1 < n2)
        return (n1);
    return (n2);
}
```

In this program, we define a function template that expects one type parameter, represented by the place-holder **num** specified between angle-brackets after the **template** keyword. On the first call to **min**:

```
min(i1, i2)
```

an instance of the function template is created. This process is said to *instantiate* a *template function*. The resulting template function has the type of the two arguments, **int**, substituted for the placeholder **num** and compares two integers. On the second call to **min**:

```
min(d1, d2)
```

a second template function is instantiated. This function has **double** substituted for **num** and compares two double floating-point numbers. The program's input-output sequence is this:

```
Enter two integers: 3 4
minimum is: 3
Enter two doubles: 3.5 4.5
minimum is: 3.5
```

You should be able to see that the compiler instantiates two template functions called **min**. In general, template functions are instantiated when the function is called or its address taken. The types of the arguments used in the function call determine which template function is instantiated:

```
min(i1, i2);
```

This causes a template function to be instantiated with the type parameter **num** becoming **int**.

Function template parameter list

In the function template declaration:

```
template<class  num>
num min(num n1, num n2);
```

<class num> is the template's formal parameter list. The keyword **class** in this context means *type parameter following*. The type parameter may be any basic or user-defined type. You must always use the **class** keyword in a template parameter list. If there is more than one type parameter, **class** must be used for each. Each parameter in the list must be unique and appear at least once in the argument list of the function. To illustrate, let's modify the **min** template:

```
//    legal template
template<class num1, class num2>
num min(num1 n1, num2 n2)
{
    //
}

//    illegal, missing class
template<class num1,  num2>
num min(num1 n1, num2 n2)

//    illegal, duplication
template<class num1, class num1, class num2>
num min(num1 n1, num2 n2)

//    illegal, num3 not used
template<class num1, class num2, class num3>
num min(num1 n1, num2 n2)
```

The names of the template type parameters don't have to match in the template declaration and definition:

```
//    declaration
template<class x, class y, class z>
num min(x n1, y n2, z n3);

//    definition
template<class num1, class num2, class num3>
num min(num1 n1, num2 n2, num3 n3)
{
    //
}
```

Declaration and definition

You must declare, if not also define, a function template at a point in the code before a template function is instantiated. If you do this, you can define the template later (see the **min** example above). As with any ordinary function, a function template's definition is its declaration if the definition precedes the first function call. The first call to the function following the definition instantiates a template function.

Both the declaration and definition of a function template must be in global scope. A template cannot be declared as a member of a class.

User-defined argument types

You can use class types, as well as other user-defined types, in the parameter list of a function template and in a call to a template function. If you do this, you must overload basic operators used within the template function on class arguments. Here's an example:

```
#include   <iostream.h>

class coord
{
private:
    int  x_coord;
    int  y_coord;
public:
    coord(int  x,  int  y)
    {
        x_coord  =  x;
        y_coord  =  y;
    }
    int  GetX()  {  return(x_coord);  }
    int  GetY()  {  return(y_coord);  }
    int  operator<(coord&  c2);
};

template<class  obj>
obj&  min(obj&  o1,  obj&  o2);          function template declaration

int  main()
{
    coord  c1(5,10);
```

```
        coord  c2(6,11);
        coord c3 = min(c1, c2);
        cout << "minimum coord is: " << c3.GetX() << " " << c3.GetY() <<
endl;

        double d1 = 3.14159;
        double d2 = 2.71828;

           cout << "minimum double is: " << min(d1, d2) << endl;
        return(0);
}
template<class obj>
obj& min(obj& o1, obj& o2)
{
        if (o1 < o2)
        return (o1);
        return (o2);
}

int coord::operator<(coord&  c2)
{
     if (x_coord < c2.x_coord)
        if (y_coord < c2.y_coord)
             return (1);
     return (0);
}
```

> compare coord objects in **min**, using overloaded < operator

> compare double objects in using basic < operator

> < operator overloaded if function instantiated for class type, otherwise built-in < used

> define overloaded < operator

We declare a class **coord**. The **min** function, if instantiated for the **coord** type, must find the minimum of two objects of type **coord**. To do this, the basic < operator must be overloaded in the **coord** class. We define and initialise two **coord** objects, **c1** and **c2**. The call:

```
coord c3 = min(c1, c2);
```

instantiates a **min** template function for the **coord** type and assigns the lesser of the two coordinates to the **coord** object **c3**. The comparison of **c1** and **c2** is done with the overloaded <. When we call **min** with arguments of the basic type **double**, the basic < operator, rather than the overloaded version, is used to compare the double floating-point numbers. The results displayed by the program are:

```
minimum coord is: 5  10
minimum double is: 2.71828
```

Class templates

The class template is actually the generalisation of the function template. With them, you can build *collections* of objects of any type *using the same class template*. Where, in conventional C++, you could have a class of floating-point numbers *or* a class of integers, with class templates, you can define a single **number** class that caters for both.

You declare a class template by prefixing a class declaration with a template specification. This is the **template** keyword followed by a pair of angle-brackets containing one or more identifiers that represent parameterised types or constant initialising values.

Using class templates, you can declare and define a class in terms of any type. Such a class is said to be parameterised. If classes generalise objects, then class templates can be said to generalise classes. Let's look at the code implementing our generic **number** class:

```
//    class template declaration
template <class numtype>
class number;

      ...
//    definition of a class instance
number<int> ni;

      ...
//    class template definition
template <class numtype>
class number
{
private:
    numtype n;
public:
    number()
    {
        n = 0;
    }
    void get_number() { cin >> n; }
    void print_number() { cout << n << endl; }
};
```

In this situation, with conventional C++, you'd usually have to take the 'brute force' approach and declare a class type for every type of number that you need. With the class template shown, you can instantiate that class for a number of any type. Instantiation occurs when the template name is used with its list of parameters. You define an instance of the class for integer numbers like this:

```
number<int>  ni;
```

Now the identifier **ni** is a class object of type **number<int>** that specifies the characteristics of an integer number. The definition causes the built-in type specifier **int** to be substituted for the class template parameter **numtype** and to be used thereafter in the class declaration in place of **numtype**. This is exactly as if you explicitly made the class declaration:

```
class  number
{
private:
    int  n;
public:
    number()
    {
        n = 0;
    }
    void  get_number() { cin >> n; }
    void  print_number() { cout << n << endl; }
};
```

and defined the instance **ni** in the ordinary way:

```
number  ni;
```

Number class template

Here's the full **number** class program:

```
#include  <iostream.h>

template  <class  numtype>
class  number
{
private:
    numtype  n;
public:
    number()
    {
        n = 0;
    }
```

134

```
        void get_number() { cin >> n; }
        void print_number() { cout << n << endl; }
};

int main()
{
    number<char>  nc;
    cout << "Enter a character: ";
    nc.get_number();
    cout << "Character is: ";
    nc.print_number();

    number<int>  ni;
    cout << "Enter an integer: ";
    ni.get_number();
    cout << "Integer is: ";
    ni.print_number();

    number<double>  nd;
    cout << "Enter a double: ";
    nd.get_number();
    cout << "Double is: ";
    nd.print_number();

    return(0);
}
```

Instantiate an integer number

Instantiate a fractional number

We make three template class instantiations, for **char**, **int** and **double** types, defining the private member **n** in turn as **char**, **int** and **double**.

The member function **get_number** extracts a value from the standard input stream and stores it in **n**. The first time it's called, **cin** uses the extractor that has a standard overloading for type **char** and expects a character to be input. On the second call to **get_number**, **cin** expects input of an **int** and on the third call a **double**. If you don't input the numbers in this order, the input operation fails. When you run the program, you get this input-output sequence:

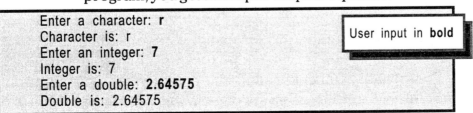

```
Enter a character: r
Character is: r
Enter an integer: 7
Integer is: 7
Enter a double: 2.64575
Double is: 2.64575
```

User input in **bold**

Class template syntax

The syntax of class templates appears daunting. While it sure ain't easy, all template syntax has an equivalent usage for simple classes. The basic equivalence is this:

```
number<int>    ni;    //    instance of template class
number         ni;    //    instance of non-template class number
```

For the template declaration **template<class numtype> class number;** the class name **number** is a parameterised type and **numtype** (when replaced by a type specifier) is its parameter. Therefore:

```
number<double>
```

is a type specifier that you can use to define a **double** instance of the template class **number** in any part of the program for which the template is in scope. Within the template definition, you can use the type specifier **number** as a shorthand for **number<numtype>**. Outside the template definition, the type specifier must be used in its full form. If you define the function **get_number** outside rather than within the template, you must use this function declaration and definition:

```
//    function declaration in template
void   get_number();
//    function definition externally
template <class  numtype>
void    number<numtype>::get_number()
{
    cin >> n;
}
```

and the definition is, of course, that of a function template, which we saw in the last section. The header syntax is complex but may make sense when we see that the equivalent non-template header is:

```
void    number::get_number()
```

You must prefix the definition of the template function **get_number** with the template specification **template<class numtype>** and specify it as being in the scope of the type **number<numtype>**.

Class templates obey the normal scope and access rules that apply to all other C++ class and data objects. You must define them in file scope (never within a function) and make them unique in a program. Class template definitions must not be nested.

Class template parameter list

In the class template declaration:

```
template<class   numtype>
class   number;
```

<class numtype> is the template's formal parameter list. The keyword **class** in this context means *type parameter following*. The type parameter may be any C++ basic or user-defined type. You must use the **class** keyword for each type specified in a parameter list. If there is more than one type parameter, **class** must be used for each parameter.

A class template parameter list can also contain *expression parameters*, usually numeric values. The arguments supplied to these parameters on instantiation of a template class must be constant expressions. The class template parameter list must not be empty and, if there is more than one parameter, the parameters must be individually separated by commas:

```
template  <class T1, int exp1, class T2>
class   someclass
{
    //
};
```

The **someclass** template specifies an expression as its second parameter and type placeholders as its first and third parameters. Instantiation of **someclass** might look like this:

```
someclass<double, 500, coord> sc;
```

You can use built-in types, user-defined types and constant expressions as class template parameters. You can intermix them in any order. The parameters specified in an instantiation must, however, be in the same order and be of the same types as those specified in the template definition. For example, the following instantiation causes a compilation error:

```
someclass<double, 500U, coord> sc;
```

The error occurs because the expression parameter **int exp1** in the template definition does not match the type **(unsigned int)** of 500U.

The container class

Class templates are often used to make very general and flexible definitions of a special kind of class called the *container class*. A container class is one that defines a collection of data objects of a particular type and also defines operations that may be carried out on that collection. Typical examples of container classes are arrays and linked lists. This section builds a simple container class, defined using class templates, for an array. Here's the class template implementation of the **array** container class:

```
#include  <iostream.h>

template  <class  slottype>
class  array
{
private:
    int     size;
    slottype   *aptr;
public:
    array(int  slots = 1)
    {
        size = slots;
        aptr = new slottype[slots];
    }
    void fill_array();
    void disp_array();
    ~array() { delete [] aptr; }
};

int  main()
{
    array<char>  ac(10);
    cout << "Fill a character array" << endl;
    ac.fill_array();
    cout << "Array contents are: ";
    ac.disp_array();

    array<double>  ad(5);
    cout << "Fill a double array" << endl;
    ad.fill_array();
    cout << "Array contents are: ";
    ad.disp_array();
    return(0);
}
```

slottype is replaced by the type of array instantiated

Allocate memory for the array of slots

Instantiate a 10-element character array

Instantiate a 5-element array of fractions

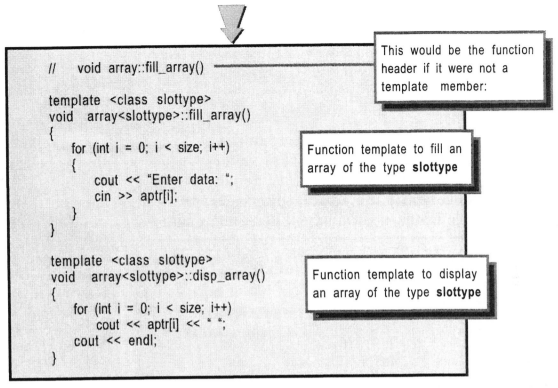

```
//     void array::fill_array()

template <class slottype>
void   array<slottype>::fill_array()
{
    for (int i = 0; i < size; i++)
    {
        cout << "Enter data: ";
        cin >> aptr[i];
    }
}

template <class slottype>
void   array<slottype>::disp_array()
{
    for (int i = 0; i < size; i++)
        cout << aptr[i] << " ";
    cout << endl;
}
```

This would be the function header if it were not a template member:

Function template to fill an array of the type **slottype**

Function template to display an array of the type **slottype**

We define a class template for the **array** class. The private data members of the class are an integer used to represent the size of the array, and a pointer to an array of objects of a type that you specify when instantiating the template class.

We also use the type parameter **slottype** in the constructor to allocate an array of the objects, which is of a size specified in the template class definition:

```
array<char>  ac(10);
```

This defines and allocates memory space for an array, called **ac**, of ten objects of type **char**.

Two class member functions, **fill_array** and **disp_array**, are then called. We declare both functions as part of the class template and define them externally.

The header of the **fill_array** function:

```
template <class slottype>
void   array<slottype>::fill_array()
```

139

specifies that the function is part of a class template with a single type parameter; that the function is in the scope of an instance of the class array defined with a type represented by **slottype**; and that the function returns no value.

When we use the **char** type to instantiate a template class, **slottype** is substituted with **char** and the **fill_array** member function operates on characters. In the second instantiation shown in the example, we use a **double** type and **fill_array** for that instance of the class operates on double floating-point numbers. Here's the program's output:

```
Fill a character array
Enter data: a
Enter data: b
Enter data: c                    ┌─────────────────────┐
Enter data: d                    │ User input in bold  │
Enter data: e                    └─────────────────────┘
Enter data: f
Enter data: g
Enter data: h
Enter data: i
Enter data: j
Array contents are: a b c d e f g h i j
Fill a double array
Enter data: 1.1
Enter data: 2.2
Enter data: 3.3
Enter data: 4.4
Enter data: 5.5
Array contents are: 1.1 2.2 3.3 4.4 5.5
```

Template hierarchies

We can derive template classes from both template and non-template classes. Here's a simple example of a hierarchy of class templates that we use to generate base and derived template classes. The example used is the array container class with the addition of a class template that uses the array class template as its base.

First, we define the base and derived class templates:

```
#include  <iostream.h>

template  <class  slottype>
class  array
{
protected:
    int   size;
    slottype  *aptr;
public:
    array(int slots = 1)
    {
        size = slots;
        aptr = new  slottype[slots];
    }
    void  fill_array();
    void  disp_array();
    ~array() { delete [] aptr; }
};

template <class  slottype>
class  term_array : public array<slottype>
{
public:
    term_array(int  slots)  :  array<slottype>(slots)
    {
    }
    void  terminate();
    void  disp_term_array();
};
```

Derived template class

We define the derived **term_array** class template with the same parameter list as **array** and with the class type **array<slottype>** publicly derived. Within the **term_array** class template, the constructor header takes a single argument, **slots**, from the instantiation of **term_array**, and passes that argument along to the constructor of the base class template **array**. You must give the type of the base class outside the scope of that class as **array<slottype>**.

Finally, the **term_array** template declares two member functions that operate on instances of the derived class template **term_array**. We define the member functions of the array class template as before:

```
template <class slottype>
void   array<slottype>::fill_array()
{
    for (int i = 0; i < size; i++)
    {
        cout << "Enter data: ";
        cin >> aptr[i];
    }
}

template <class slottype>
void   array<slottype>::disp_array()
{
    for (int i = 0; i < size; i++)
        cout << aptr[i] << " ";
    cout << endl;
}
```

We define the **term_array** member functions similarly, specifying that they are in the scope **term_array<slottype>**:

```
template <class slottype>
void   term_array<slottype>::disp_term_array()
{
    cout << "Contents of terminated array are: ";
    for (int i = 0; aptr[i] != (slottype)0 ; i++)
        cout << aptr[i] << endl;
}

template <class slottype>
void   term_array<slottype>::terminate()
{
    cout << "Null terminating the array"
            << endl;
    aptr[size] = (slottype)0;
}
```

The **main** function defines an instance of the derived class template **term_array**. It then calls the **fill_array** member function of the base class array to accept input values and to store those values in the array. This is an operation common to all arrays.

142

The characteristics of terminated arrays which are additional to those of general arrays are dealt with by the **term_array** member functions **terminate** and **disp_term_array**. The **terminate** function null-terminates the array and **disp_term_array** displays it using the insertion operator for the basic type in use.

```cpp
int main()
{
    term_array<char>   ac(10);

    cout << "Fill a character array" << endl;
    ac.fill_array();
    ac.terminate();
    ac.disp_term_array();

    array<double>   ad(5);
    cout << "Fill a double array" << endl;
    ad.fill_array();
    cout << "Array contents are: ";
    ad.disp_array();

    return(0);
}
```

Exception handling

The exception-handling mechanism provided by C++ allows you to recover from errors that may occur while your program is running. The program below shows a straightforward implementation.

```cpp
#include  <iostream.h>
void  throw_test(int);

class  ob
{
public:
    int  member;
};

int  main()
{
    int  flag = 2;
    try                          [try block]
        {
            throw_test(flag);
        }
    catch(const  char * p)
        {
            cout << "Into character catch-handler" << endl;
            cout << p << endl;
        }                                            [catch handlers]
    catch(ob&  ob_inst)
        {
            cout << "Into object catch-handler" << endl;
            cout << "Member value is " << ob_inst.member << endl;
        }
        return(0);
}

void throw_test(int  flag)
{
    if (flag == 1)
        throw  "Panic!!!";
        else
    if (flag == 2)
        {                            [The function within the try
            ob ob_inst;               block, for which exceptions
            ob_inst.member = 5;       are caught.]
            throw  ob_inst;
        }
}
```

144

We call a function, **throw_test**, from within a *try block* in **main**. The function call is the only code enclosed in the try block. If an error condition of some kind arises within **throw_test** or code called from it, an exception may be *thrown*, to be *caught* by the *catch-handlers* that immediately follow the **try** block.

In this case, the generation of 'exceptions' is contrived: if the value of the parameter **flag** received by **throw_test** is 1, an exception of type **const char *** is thrown; if the value is 2, the exception is of the class type **ob**. The two catch-handlers following the **try** block in **main** respectively match these types. If the value of **flag** is 1, **throw_test** exits by throwing the character-string exception "*Panic!!!*". The resulting program output is:

```
Into  character  catch-handler
Panic!!!
```

If the value of **flag** is 2, **throw_test** exits by throwing the **ob** exception **ob_inst**. Its only data member has the value 5 and the resulting program output is:

```
Into  object  catch-handler
Member  value  is  5
```

Nested functions in the try block

The catch-handlers invoked by the exceptions thrown from the function **throw_test** in the last example are also invoked by exceptions thrown from a function indirectly called from **throw_test**.

```cpp
#include  <iostream.h>

void  nest1(int);
void  nest2(int);
void  throw_test(int);

class  ob
{
public:
    int  member;
};
```

```
int main()
{
    int flag = 1;
    try
    {
        throw_test(flag);
    }
    catch(const char * p)
    {
        cout << "Into character catch-handler" << endl;
        cout << p << endl;
    }
    catch(ob& ob_inst)
    {
        cout << "Into object catch-handler" << endl;
        cout << "Member value is " << ob_inst.member << endl;
    }
    return(0);
}

void throw_test(int flag)
{
    nest1(flag);
}

void nest1(int flag)
{
    nest2(flag);
}

void nest2(int flag)
{
    if (flag == 1)
        throw "Panic!!!";
        else
    if (flag == 2)
    {
        ob ob_inst;
        ob_inst.member = 5;

        throw ob_inst;
    }
}
```

try block

Nested functions also governed by **try** block.

In this case, **throw_test** calls **nest1**, which in turn calls **nest2**. All three functions are subject to the **try** block and the exceptions thrown from **nest2** are caught by the catch handlers following that block. The output results of the program are the same as those for the previous example.

Catch-handler selection

The matching catch handlers closest to the thrown exceptions are those invoked, as we can see from the following example:

```cpp
#include  <iostream.h>

void  nest1(int);
void  nest2(int);
void  throw_test(int);

class  ob
{
public:
    int  member;
};

int  main()
{
    int  flag = 1;
    try
    {
        throw_test(flag);
    }
    catch(const  char * p)
    {
        cout << "Into 'main' character catch-handler" << endl;
        cout << p << endl;
    }
    catch(ob&  ob_inst)
    {
        cout << "Into object catch-handler" << endl;
        cout << "Member value is " << ob_inst.member << endl;
    }

    return(0);
}
```

```
void throw_test(int flag)
{
    try
    {
        nest1(flag);
    }
    catch(const char * p)
    {
        cout << "Into 'throw_test' character catch-handler" << endl;
        cout << p << endl;
    }
}

void nest1(int flag)
{
    nest2(flag);
}

void nest2(int flag)
{
    if (flag == 1)
        throw "Panic!!!";
        else
    if (flag == 2)
    {
        ob ob_inst;
        ob_inst.member = 5;
        throw ob_inst;
    }
}
```

> This catch-handler used before the one in **main**.

Here both **main** and **throw_test** contain **try** blocks, while the nested function **nest2** generates the exceptions. If **nest2** throws a character-string exception, the matching catch-handler in **throw_test** is invoked. If it throws an exception of type **ob**, the effect is to call the second catch-handler in **main**. Here are the output results of the program:

```
Into 'throw_test' character catch-handler
Panic!!!
```

Finally, **throw** used without an exception specification:

```
throw;
```

causes the most recently thrown exception to be re-thrown to the catch handlers following the nearest **try** block.

148

Namespaces

The namespace is a scope specification introduced in ANSI C++. Its purpose is to eliminate the kind of name clashes that are common in large ISO C and pre-ANSI C++ programs.

The ISO C language specifies three levels of scope:

- File (translation unit).
- Function (goto-label).
- Local (enclosing block).

Traditional C++ introduced one more, the class scope.

Variables and functions declared and defined in file scope are commonly referred to as global variables. The more formal name for a program file is translation unit. If we define a variable in one translation unit:

```
int glob = 5;
```

it is accessed in another translation unit by means of an **extern** declaration:

```
extern int glob;
```

and, if **glob** has not been assigned to after its initialisation, it will in the second translation unit have the value 5. The C++ class scope makes necessary use of the scope-resolution operator, ::, as explained in Chapter 2:

```
class ob
{
public:
    void func();
};

void ob::func()
{
    //
}
```

None of the levels of scope referred to deals with the problem of the global name clash, exemplified by the case of two header files containing similar declarations that you may want to include in the same translation unit:

```
// header1.h
class ob
{
public:
    int x;
};
int func(int);
int func(double);

// header2.h
class ob
{
public:
    double x;
    void f();
};
int func(int);
```

If you use the two header files in the same program file, you get
clashes between the declarations of the class **ob** and the prototypes
of the functions **func**. The solution adopted is the **namespace** scope
specification coupled with the **using** declaration:

```
// header1.h
namespace ns1
{
class ob
{
public:
    int x;
};
int func(int);
int func(double);
}

// header2.h
namespace ns2
{
class ob
{
public:
    double x;
    void f();
};
int func(int);
}
```

We define the function **func** declared in the scope of namespace **ns1** like this:

```
void ns1::f()
{
    //
}
```

and thereby distinguish it from the **func** referenced in namespace **ns2**. Equally, the class objects can be distinguished. To define an instance of **ob** as declared in namespace **ns2**, we use any of the three forms:

```
ns2::ob  ob_inst;
```

or

```
using ns2::ob;   // now using ob as declared in ns2
ob ob_inst; // define instance of  ns2::ob
```

or

```
using namespace ns2; // all ns2 names now current
ob ob_inst;        // define instance of ns2::ob
ns2::func();       // call func as declared by ns2
```

Namespaces are an elegant solution to a problem that has existed since the inception of the C language. They can be viewed as a generalisation of the class-scope specification.

Run time type identification

The most recent major extension to the C++ language as it was originally conceived is run time type identification, (*RTTI*). In essence, you apply the facilities of RTTI to a given class instance to determine its type. The typical usages are:

- checking that a pointer is of a type derived from a given base type

- identifying the actual type of a pointer.

RTTI should be used sparingly and with care. The whole point of the inheritance and virtual function mechanisms described in Chapter 4 is that you *need not* know the type of a derived-class pointer in order to use it to call a virtual member function of that derived class. RTTI runs contrary to polymorphism and it's easy to use it badly, allowing degeneration into an alternative form of multi-way **switch** construct:

```
if (typeid(d1) == typeid(supervisor))
    cout << "It's a supervisor" << endl;
else
if (typeid(d1) == typeid(manager))
    cout << "It's a manager" << endl;
else
if (typeid(d1) == typeid(lineManager))
    cout << "It's a line manager" << endl;
```

Using RTTI is OK where, for a particular type of derived class, an exception needs to be made. The problem inherent in this can be stated: "Given a base class pointer previously assigned an unknown value, how can we ascertain that it points to an instance of the base class or one of its derived classes and, further, how can we determine its actual type?" The answer in both cases, with traditional C++, is that we can't. Enter RTTI.

Identifying derived class objects

To illustrate RTTI, we use a modified form of the **employee** class hierarchy introduced earlier. From the **main** function, we pass a base class pointer as an argument to a global function. That function must determine whether or not the pointer holds a pointer value of derived-class type. If it does, then in the case of **managers**, the employee is paid. Striking **supervisor**s, on the other hand, are not paid.

152

```
    enum  qualification  {NONE,  CERT,  DIPLOMA,  DEGREE,  POSTGRAD};

    class  employee
    {
    protected:
        char *name;
        char *dateOfBirth;
        int  individualEmployeeNo;
        static int employeeNo;
        int grade;
        qualification  employeeQual;
        float accumPay;
    public:
        employee();  // constructor
        ~employee(); // destructor
        virtual void pay();
        void promote(int);         // scale increment
        void  displayStatus();
    };

    class supervisor : public employee
    {
    private:
        float  monthlyPay;
    public:
        supervisor();    // constructor
        ~supervisor();    // destructor
        void pay();
        void  displayStatus();
    };

    class manager : public employee
    {
    private:
        float  monthlyPay;
        float  bonus;
    public:
        manager();   // constructor
        ~manager(); // destructor
        void pay();
        void  displayStatus();
    };

    void  pay_managers_only(employee  *);
```

Global function to demonstrate RTTI

empfunc.cpp (functions)

```cpp
#include  <iostream.h>
#include  <string.h>
#include  "employee.h"

//       define and initialise static member
int  employee::employeeNo  =  1000;

employee::employee()
{
    char  nameIn[50];
    cout  <<  "Enter new employee name ";
    cin  >>  nameIn;
    name  =  new char[strlen(nameIn) + 1];
    strcpy(name,  nameIn);
    dateOfBirth  =  NULL;
    individualEmployeeNo  =  employeeNo++;
    grade  =  1;
    employeeQual  =  NONE;
    accumPay  =  0.0;
}
employee::~employee()
{
    delete  name;
    delete  dateOfBirth;
}
void  employee::pay()
{
}
void  employee::promote(int  increment)
{
    grade  +=  increment;
}
void  employee::displayStatus()
{
}

supervisor::supervisor()
{
    monthlyPay  =  1700.00;
    cout  <<  "Supervisor "  <<  name  <<  " is hired"  <<  endl;
}
```

Define 'employee' member functions first

Define 'supervisor' member functions

```cpp
supervisor::~supervisor()
{
    cout << "Supervisor " << name << " is fired!" << endl;
}
void  supervisor::pay()
{
    accumPay  += monthlyPay;
    cout << "Supervisor " << individualEmployeeNo
         << " paid " << monthlyPay << endl;

}
void   supervisor::displayStatus()
{
    cout << "Supervisor " << individualEmployeeNo
         << " is of grade " << grade << " and has been paid "
         << accumPay << " so far this year" << endl;

}

manager::manager()
{
    monthlyPay = 2100.00;
    bonus      = 210.0;
    cout << "Manager " << name << " is hired" << endl;
}
manager::~manager()
{
    cout << "Manager " << name << " is fired!" << endl;

}
void   manager::pay()
{
    accumPay  += monthlyPay;
    cout << "Manager " << individualEmployeeNo
         << " paid " << monthlyPay << endl;

}
void   manager::displayStatus()
{
    cout << "Manager " << individualEmployeeNo
         << " is of grade " << grade << " and has been paid "
         << accumPay << " so far this year" << endl;

}
```

Define 'manager' member functions

```
#include  <iostream.h>
#include  "employee.h"

int  main()
{
    supervisor  s1;
    manager     m1;
    employee    *ep = &s1;
    pay_managers_only(ep);
    ep = &m1;
    pay_managers_only(ep);
    return(0);
}

void  pay_managers_only(employee  *base)
{
    manager  *mp;
    supervisor  *sp;
    if ((mp = dynamic_cast<manager *>(base)) != 0)
        base->pay();
    else
    if ((sp = dynamic_cast<supervisor *>(base)) != 0)
        cout << "Don't pay striking supervisors" << endl;
    else
        cout << "Unknown employee type" << endl;
}
```

The interesting part of this example is here, in the client code, **main** and the function it calls.

From **main, pay_managers_only** is twice called with a base class pointer (of type **employee**) as argument. On entering the function, no way exists in traditional C++ of determining the type of **base**. Using RTTI, we do this using the *dynamic cast* mechanism:

```
    if ((sp = dynamic_cast<supervisor *>(base)) != 0)
```

If the contents of the pointer **base** refer to a base or derived object, that pointer is dynamically typecast and assigned to **sp**. Otherwise, **sp** is assigned zero. In the example, on the first call (for **supervisors**) to **pay_managers_only**, the virtual **pay** function is not called, while on the second call it is. The program's displayed output shown below:

```
Enter new employee name susan
Supervisor susan is hired
Enter new employee name peter
Manager peter is hired
Don't pay striking supervisors
Manager 1001 paid 2100
Manager peter is fired!
Supervisor susan is fired!
```

As well as comparing with the base class type, you can determine the precise type of an object. The **typeid()** operator yields the actual type, not just that a given object is or is not of a type included in a class hierarchy. A simple example of **typeid()** in use is given below.

emp.cpp (program)

```cpp
#include  <iostream.h>
#include  <typeinfo.h>
#include  "employee.h"

int  main()
{
    supervisor  s1;
    manager     m1;
    employee    *ep = &s1;
    pay_managers_only(ep);
    ep = &m1;
    pay_managers_only(ep);
    return(0);
}

void  pay_managers_only(employee  *base)
{
    if (typeid(*base)  ==  typeid(manager))
        base->pay();
}
```

> The internal specification of **type_info** is implementation-dependent but it minimally provides overloaded assignment and **==** operators, as well as a function to return a character pointer to the name of the type found in the call to **typeid()**.

The **main** function is unchanged. **pay_managers_only** now does an explicit comparison of types in deciding whether or not to pay the employee. **typeid()** returns a reference to library class **type_info**. This class is declared in the standard header file **typeinfo.h**, which must be included for the **type_info** data to be accessible in client code.

Exercises

1. Write down the declaration of a class template **array\<arraytype\>**. Make instantiations of template classes for the **int**, **char** and **double** types.

   Show how a member function is declared within the class template and defined externally.

2. Declare and define a function template called **max** that you can use to find the maximum of two objects of *any* type. For non-numeric objects, what might **max** mean? Show how overloading can be used to define this.

6 The C++ library

Introduction

ANSI C++ introduces the C++ Library. This is an enormously-expanded set of facilities that provides services including standard templates, container classes, string-handling classes and others.

This chapter concentrates on the Stream I/O (file input-output) library. The Stream I/O library and with associated header files are an alternative to the C Standard I/O functions declared in **stdio.h**.

Stream I/O is implemented as a hierarchy of classes. The base class is a stream, which may represent a file on disk, a peripheral device such as a terminal or printer, or some other system device. It may be an input stream, output stream or one capable of both input and output.

The base stream class also defines the low-level operations that can be carried out on the stream. You don't see these low-level operations; as a user of the classes, you only need to know how to use the interface provided by higher-level I/O functions declared in classes derived from the base. These functions include **get** and **read** for use on input streams and **put** and **write** for use on output streams.

One of the benefits of Stream I/O and of C++ in general is that the interface presented to the programmer does not change with data type. Suppose we have a data object **X** of one of the types **char**, **int**, **float** and **double**, but we don't know which it is, then the statement:

    cout << X;

using the Stream I/O operator **<<**, correctly sends to the output stream the value of **X**. On the other hand, the C statement:

    printf("%d", X);

fails if **X** is, for instance, of type **double**. There's no easy way in C of implementing functions that operate correctly on arbitrary types. Stream I/O functions and operators do this in a *type safe* manner by using the function- and operator-overloading capabilities. Stream I/O in these ways provides a uniform programmer interface and eliminates some of the more piecemeal aspects of the C Standard I/O library.

The Stream I/O class hierarchy is declared in the header files **iostream.h**, **fstream.h** and **iomanip.h**, which collectively replace

stdio.h. C++ implements the standard I/O streams with the following instances of classes declared in the Stream I/O class hierarchy:

```
cin    Standard input
cout   Standard output
cerr   Standard error
clog   Buffered cerr for voluminous error text
```

The operators << for output and >> for input are overloaded. The << operator overloaded for stream output is called the *insertion operator* or *inserter*. When used, it is said to insert bytes on the output stream. The >> operator overloaded for stream input is called the *extraction operator* or *extractor*. When used, it is said to extract bytes from the input stream.

The extractor and inserter operators are basic C++ bit-shift operators overloaded to have multiple definitions as operator functions. The multiple overloadings allow you to use the operators for input and output of objects of many different data types; they, not you, take care of type-safety.

Here's a highly simplified diagram of the Stream I/O class hierarchy with a short summary of the relevant functions and operators that are members of the various classes:

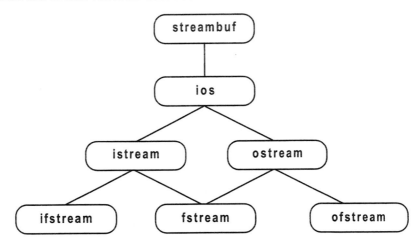

The **streambuf** class is declared in the header file **iostream.h**. It describes the stream buffer object and defines low-level I/O operations.

Usually, you don't have to be concerned with the definitions in the **streambuf** class or the details of the low-level I/O performed by it.

The **ios** (I/O state) class, also declared in **iostream.h**, inherits **streambuf** and contains more information about the state of the stream. This includes the stream open mode, seek direction and format flags. The following functions are also declared in the **ios** class:

flags	setf	unsetf	width	fill	precision	
tie	rdstate	eof	fail	bad	good	clear

The functions in the first row are for data formatting and are explained in the next section.

From **ios** are derived the input stream **istream** and output stream **ostream** classes. These declare I/O functions and operators that are used by the C++ programmer. Both **istream** and **ostream** are declared in the header file **iostream.h**. **istream** contains function declarations including the following:

get	peek	read	putback
getline	seekg	gcount	tellg

The class **ostream** includes these function declarations:

put	seekp	write	tellp

istream also contains the definitions of the overloaded extractor >>, while **ostream** contains the definitions for the inserter <<.

The class **iostream** inherits both **istream** and **ostream**. It is declared in **iostream.h**. The file I/O classes **ifstream** and **ofstream** are declared in the header file **fstream.h**. **ifstream** inherits all the standard input stream operations defined by **istream** and adds a few more, such as constructors and functions for opening files. **ofstream** similarly augments the inherited definitions of **ostream**.

Finally, **fstream**, declared in the header file **fstream.h**, inherits **iostream** and contains functions and constructors that allow files to be opened in input-output mode.

Formatted I/O

All Stream I/O done in earlier chapters is unformatted: the formats of output and input data are default settings used by the insertion and extraction operators. You can specify these formats explicitly:

- The **setf**, **unsetf** and **flags** functions use format flags to alter input and output data. The **ios** class enumerates the flag values and also declares the functions.

- The **ios** class member functions **width**, **precision** and **fill**, are used to set the format of input and output data.

- Using manipulators, special functions that combine the above two techniques and add some more.

Format flags

Every C++ input and output stream has defined for it (in the **ios** base class) a number of format flags that determine the appearance of input and output data. They are represented in bit form in a long integer and are defined as an enumerated type within the class **ios** as follows:

```
class ios
{
public:
    // formatting flags
    enum
    {
        // skip white space on input
        skipws= 0x0001,
        // left-adjust output
        left    = 0x0002,
        // right-adjust output
        right      = 0x0004,
        // pad after sign or base indicator
        internal   = 0x0008,
        // decimal conversion
        dec        = 0x0010,
        // octal conversion
        oct     = 0x0020,
        // hexadecimal conversion
        hex        = 0x0040,
```

```
            // show integer base on output
            showbase= 0x0080,
            // show decimal point and trailing zeros
            showpoint= 0x0100,
            // uppercase hex output
            uppercase  = 0x0200,
            // explicit + with positive integers
            showpos  = 0x0400,
            // scientific notation
            scientific = 0x0800,
            // floating notation (e.g. 123.45)
            fixed      = 0x1000,
            // flush output after each output operation
            unitbuf= 0x2000,
            // flush output after each character inserted
            stdio      = 0x4000
      };
   };
```

Here's an example of how to use format flags. We define an integer and initialise it to a decimal value. We then write it to the standard output in its hexadecimal form, showing the base (**0X**) in uppercase:

```
int number = 45;
// set uppercase hexadecimal and show the base
cout.setf(ios::hex | ios::showbase | ios::uppercase);
cout << number << endl;
```

In this example, the trailing newline output to **cout** is replaced by **endl**. You saw this first in Chapter 1. **endl** is a manipulator that has the effect of inserting a newline on the stream and flushing the stream. The output of the code is this:

```
0X2D
```

The bit values of the **ios** flags **hex**, **showbase** and **uppercase** are combined using the logical **OR** statement and used as the argument to the **setf** member function of the **cout** stream. The format flags set in this way cause all subsequent integers written to the standard output to be displayed in hexadecimal, until the flags are changed or unset. You switch the flags off using the **unsetf** function:

```
cout.unsetf(ios::hex | ios::showbase | ios::uppercase);
```

After this operation, the output format reverts to what it was before the call to **setf**. Here are the prototypes of the **setf**, **unsetf** and **flags** functions:

```
long  setf(long);
long  setf(long,  long);
long  unsetf(long);
long  flags();
long  flags(long);
```

The function **setf** called with a single argument of type **long** turns on the format flags specified in that argument. **setf** returns the format flag values as they were before the call to **setf**. An overloaded definition of **setf** takes two **long** arguments. A call to this function turns off the flags specified by the second argument and then turns on the flags specified by the first. The function returns the format flag values as they were before it was called.

The function **unsetf** turns off the flags specified by its argument and returns the format flag values as they were before **unsetf** was called.

A call to the **flags** function without arguments returns the current state of the format flags. The **flags** function called with one **long** argument sets the format flags to the values specified by that argument and returns the values of the flags as they were before the call to **flags**. This function is important in being the only one of the five shown that actually clears all previous format flag settings.

Manipulating format flags

This program uses the flag-setting functions and some of the flags.

```
#include  <iostream.h>

int main()
{
    long old_flags;   // old flag values
    long tmp_flags;   // temporary flag values
    long new_flags;   // new flag values
    int number  = 45;
```

```
//    store original format flag values
old_flags = cout.flags();

//    show + sign if positive
cout.setf(ios::showpos);
cout << number << endl;

//    set uppercase hexadecimal and show the base
new_flags = ios::hex | ios::showbase |
                          ios::uppercase;
tmp_flags = cout.setf(new_flags);
cout << number << endl;

//    display twice to show that setf is persistent
cout << number << endl;

//    unset the uppercase flag
cout.unsetf(ios::uppercase);
cout << number << endl;

//    revert to showpos only
cout.setf(tmp_flags,  new_flags);
cout << number << endl;

//    return to original format flag values
new_flags = cout.flags(old_flags);
cout << number << endl;
return(0);
}
```

This is the output when the program is run:

```
+45
0X2D
0X2D
0x2d
+45
45
```

Because the individual flag values are members of the **ios** class, they must be scope-resolved when they are used: **ios::hex** is correct, while **hex** alone is not.

Where a number of flags are to be used as arguments to **setf**, **unsetf** or **flags**, first assign them to a long integer and use that as the argument:

```
new_flags = ios::hex | ios::showbase | ios::uppercase;
tmp_flags = cout.setf(new_flags);
```

These are the characteristics of the other format flags:

- **dec** is used to control the number base, converting output integers to decimal and causing input integers to be treated as decimal; it is the default base value.

- **skipws**, if set (which is the default), causes white space to be skipped on input using the extraction operator.

- **left** and **right** cause field-justification with padding by a fill character; right is the default.

- **internal** causes the fill character to be inserted between any leading sign or base and the value.

- **showpoint** causes a decimal point and trailing zeros to be output for floating-point numbers, whether they are needed or not.

- **scientific** causes floating-point display to be of the form:

  ```
  m.ppppppex
  ```

  where **m** is a digit, followed by a decimal point and a number of digits to a precision specified by the current precision value (see **precision()** below). The default precision is **6**. The decimals are followed either by **e** or **E** (the latter if **ios::fixed** is set) and an exponent. The value:

  ```
  3141.592654
  ```

  displayed in scientific form is:

  ```
  3.141593e03
  ```

- **fixed** causes floating-point values to be displayed in normal (non-scientific) notation.

- **unitbuf** and **stdio**, when set, cause the output buffers to be flushed after each output operation and output character respectively.

Field width and precision

You can use the **ios** class member functions **width**, **precision** and **fill** to do further formatting on input or output data. Here's an example program which exercises all three functions:

```cpp
#include  <iostream.h>

int main()
{
    double pi = 3.141592654;

    //   default display is left-justified with precision 6
    cout << pi << endl;

    //   set precision 4, field width 12 and fill character +
    cout.precision(4);
    cout.width(12);
    cout.fill('+');

    cout << pi << endl;

    //   width setting is not persistent, fill setting is

    cout.width(12);
    cout << pi << endl;

    //   precision without argument keeps previous value
    cout << "Current precision: " << cout.precision() <<  endl;
    cout.precision(8);

    //   width does not truncate
    cout.width(2);
    cout.fill('-');
    cout << pi << endl;
    return(0);
}
```

These are the output results of the program:

```
3.141593
++++++3.1416
++++++3.1416
Current precision: 4
3.14159265
```

168

Stream output and input

Stream output

Stream I/O provides the insertion (stream output) operator overloaded to handle a number of data types. These are referred to as built-in insertion types. Overloading of the insertion operator is done according to the rules of operator overloading (see Chapter 4). This short program illustrates how the insertion operator is overloaded:

```
#include  <iostream.h>

int main()
{
    float f = 2.71828;
    cout << f;
    cout.operator<<(f);
    return(0);
}
```

The insertion operations on **cout** are equivalent and identical in their effect. In the second, full form, the operator function **operator<<** is explicitly called for the output stream **cout. operator<<** returns a reference to a class (stream) object of the type with which it is called, in this case **ostream**. This allows you to chain insertion operations:

```
cout << "Value of e is: " << f << endl;
```

Here are the built-in Stream I/O inserter types for output:

```
char (signed and unsigned)
short (signed and unsigned)
int (signed and unsigned)
long (signed and unsigned)
const char * (string)
float
double
long double
void * (void pointer, hex address)
```

You can, if you're sufficiently motivated, define further overloaded operator functions for insertion. These are of the same form and behaviour as the built-in inserters. For details on customised inserters, I refer you to the *Newnes C++ Pocket Book*.

Functions

There are two functions, in addition to the inserters, for simple output to a stream. The **put** member function of the **ostream** class writes a single character to an output stream. Its lone prototype is:

```
ostream&  put(char);
```

The class **ostream** contains a member function **flush**, with this prototype:

```
ostream&  flush();
```

Using of **flush** has the effect of flushing and writing the contents of the buffered stream for which it is called:

```
cout.flush();      // function  call
```

Stream input

The facilities provided by Stream I/O for input are symmetrical to those for output. The overloaded extraction operator **>>** is used for stream input. Extractors share many characteristics with inserters:

- Extractors, like inserters, are overloaded operator functions.
- You can chain extraction operations in the same way as insertion operations.
- You can use an extractor on any input stream; there is no concept of separate operations for different streams, along the lines of **scanf** and **fscanf** in the C Standard Library.
- As with inserters, you can customise your own extractors. As with inserters also, for this, see the *Newnes C++ Pocket Book*.

The following are the built-in Stream I/O inserter types for input:

```
char (signed  and  unsigned)
short (signed  and  unsigned)
int   (signed  and unsigned)
long (signed  and  unsigned)
char  *  (string)
float
double
long  double
```

Extraction operations that accept input from the standard I/O stream **cin** by default, skip leading white spaces and white-space-separated input. This can be changed with the **skipws** format flag or the **ws** manipulator (see the example below). Extraction fails if data of a type not matching the receiving variables is received.

Functions

Stream I/O provides a number of functions, in addition to the inserters already described, for simple input from a stream. The **get** function has a number of overloadings allowing different definitions of the function to perform different tasks on an input stream. These are the **get** prototypes:

```
int     get();
istream&  get(char&);
istream&  get(char *, int l, char d = \n);
```

Given these definitions:

```
char  c;
int  i;
char  carr[20];
```

and extracting from the input stream, **cin**, the following calls to get are valid:

```
i = cin.get();       // read one character, white space or not

cin.get(c);          // read one character, white space or not

cin.get(carr,20);  // get at most 20 characters into the array carr until
                     // default newline seen but not read from the stream
```

The **peek** function has only one definition. Its prototype is:

```
int  peek();
```

peek looks ahead at, without reading, the next character on the input stream.

This is the prototype of **putback**:

```
istream&  putback(char);
```

putback pushes an already-read character back onto the input stream; it will be read by the next input operation.

The **getline** function is equivalent to the third definition of **get** above, except that it also reads the delimiter which is, by default, a newline character. **get** leaves the delimiter on the input stream. This is the prototype of **getline**:

```
istream& getline(char* b, int len, char d = \n);
```

getline reads at most **len** characters, delimited by the character **d** or by default a newline, into the array pointed to by **b**.

The **gcount** function returns the number of characters read by the last read operation on an input stream. Its prototype is this:

```
int gcount();
```

The **ignore** function is similar to a **flush** function for an input stream. (No input-stream **flush** function is defined in Stream I/O.) This is its prototype:

```
istream& ignore(int len = 1, int d = EOF);
```

When you call **ignore**, it discards up to **len** characters (default value 1) or until a delimiter character is encountered on the input stream. The delimiter character is also discarded.

File I/O

Using Stream I/O, you open a file by linking it with an input, output or input-output stream. You do this either by explicitly calling the stream member function **open** or allowing the stream constructor to open the file implicitly. A file is closed by disassociating it from its stream. This is done either explicitly by the stream member function **close** or implicitly by the stream destructor.

To use files under Stream I/O, you must include the **fstream.h** header file. **fstream.h** includes the three classes **ifstream**, **ofstream** and **fstream**, for input, output and input-output files respectively. These classes declare all the functions needed to access files in input, output and input-output modes.

Before a file can be opened, you must define an object of the required stream type:

```
ifstream ins;
```

Then you can open the file:

```
ins.open("infile");
```

You can alternatively open the file automatically using the **ifstream** constructor:

```
ifstream ins("infile");
```

If the file **infile** does not exist, it is created. When the file has been opened, the stream object **ins** keeps track of the current state of the file: its size; open mode; access characteristics; current position of the read pointer; and error conditions, if any. You can close the file explicitly using the stream member function **close**:

```
ins.close();
```

or else rely on the **ifstream** destructor to close the file when the stream object **ins** goes out of scope.

It's OK to open a file using its name only, but there are many other options. The full prototype of the input stream **open** function, declared in the class **ifstream**, is this:

```
void open(char *n, int m = ios::in, int p = filebuf::openprot);
```

The output stream **open** function, declared in **ofstream**, has this prototype:

```
void open(char *n, int m = ios::out, int p = filebuf::openprot);
```

The input-output **open** function is declared in **fstream** as follows:

```
void open(char *n, int m, int p = filebuf::openprot);
```

The first argument in all cases is a string representing the file name; the second is the open mode; and the third the file access permissions. The open mode for input files is by default **ios::open**. For output files, it is by default **ios::out**.

Let's look at a number of examples of simple file I/O. All the examples are based around the same program, which simply copies one text file to another. To do so, we call a **filecopy** function.

Basic file copy

Here's the basic program, **filecopy.cpp**:

filecopy.cpp

```
#include  <iostream.h>
#include  <fstream.h>

void filecopy(ifstream &, ofstream &);

int main(int argc, char *argv[])
{
    if (argc != 3)
    {
        cout << "Invalid arguments specified\n";
        return(0);
    }
    ifstream fin(argv[1]);
    if (!fin)
    {
        cout << "Can not open input file\n";
        return(0);
    }
```

Check for 3 command line arguments, including program name.

Check that the input file is readable.

```
        ofstream  fout(argv[2]);
        if (!fout)
        {
            cout << "Can not open output file\n";
            return(0);
        }

        filecopy(fin, fout);
        fin.close();
        fout.close();
        return(0);
}

void filecopy(ifstream &in, ofstream &out)
{
        char c;

        while (in.get(c), !in.eof())
            out.put(c);
}
```

Copy character-by-character from input to output stream

You can execute the program by entering at the command line:

```
filecopy infile outfile
```

The file **infile** is linked to the input stream **ifstream** and opened. If for some reason it can't be opened, the stream object **fin** is set to null, an error is reported and the program stops. If the file **outfile** can't be opened, the program similarly stops. If both files are successfully opened, their associated stream objects **fin** and **fout** are supplied as reference arguments to the function **filecopy**. This function then reads characters from the input file and writes them to the output file, stopping when end-of-file is encountered on the input file. The error-state function, **eof**, declared in the class **ios**, returns TRUE on end-of-file.

In the next example, we see the files being opened using explicit **open** function calls. The output file is opened in input-output mode and, after the copy, is opened in input mode and displayed.

Only the **main** function is shown:

```cpp
#include  <iostream.h>
#include  <fstream.h>

void filecopy(ifstream &, fstream &);

int main(int argc, char *argv[])
{
    if (argc != 3)
    {
        cout << "Invalid arguments specified\n";
        return(0);
    }

    ifstream fin;
    fin.open(argv[1], ios::in);              ────────  Open for input

    if (!fin)
    {
        cout << "Can not open input file\n";
        return(0);
    }

    fstream fout;
    fout.open(argv[2], ios::out);            ────────  Open for output

    if (!fout)
    {
        cout << "Can not open output file\n";
        return(0);
    }

    filecopy(fin, fout);

    char c;
    fout.close();                            Close, open and
    fout.open(argv[2], ios::in);             read the output file
    while (fout.get(c), !fout.eof())
        cout << c;
                                             Display contents
    fin.close();                             of the output file
    fout.close();
    return(0);
}
```

If we had opened the output file in append mode with:

```
fin.open(argv[2], ios::app);
```

or:

```
fstream fin(argv[2], ios::app);
```

the contents of the input file would be added to the end of any existing output file instead of overwriting it. In the case of append mode, if the file does not already exist, it is created.

We can implement the **filecopy** function using the multi-character overloading of the **get** function. Here, I haven't changed the **main** function from the original **filecopy.cpp**. Only the **filecopy** function is shown:

```
const int MAX = 100;

void filecopy(ifstream &in, ofstream &out)
{
    char  instring[MAX];

    while (in.get(instring, MAX, \n), !in.eof())
    {
        out << instring;

        // get and copy the newline
        char c;
        c = in.peek();
        if (c == \n)
        {
            in.get(c);
            out.put(c);
        }
    }
}
```

We define a local character array, **instring**, to act as an input buffer. Then we read a line from the input file up to, but not including, the trailing newline. If we don't find a newline character, we read a maximum of 100 characters. Either way, the characters are stored in **instring**, the contents of which are then written to the output file using the built-in inserter.

At the end of each line, the newline must be processed. We do this here a little over-elaborately, the **peek** function being used to check that the next character is indeed a newline before the copy. we could do the same job in a more crude (and error-prone) way:

```
while (in.get(instring, MAX), !in.eof())
{
    out << instring;

    // get and copy the newline
    in.get();
    out.put('\n');
}
```

In this case, the **get** call uses the fact that its third argument, the delimiter, has the default value **'\n'**. We then use the version of the **get** function that takes no arguments to discard the next character after the line is read. The **put** function then writes a hard-coded newline character to the output file.

In the final variant of the **filecopy** function, we use **getline** to read the input file and **gcount** to count the characters actually read:

```
const int MAX = 100;

void filecopy(ifstream &in, ofstream &out)
{
    long total_chars = 0;
    char instring[MAX];

    while (in.getline(instring, MAX, \n), !in.eof())
    {
        total_chars += in.gcount();
        out << instring;
    }
    cout << "File copied: " << total_chars << " bytes" << endl;
}
```

getline reads from the input file a newline-terminated line, including the newline character. The built-in inserter then writes the line to the output stream. On each iteration, we increment the total number of characters actually read. At the end of the function, we report the number of characters copied.

Random file access

Some basic facilities are provided by Stream I/O for random access, that is, starting file access at any point in the file. For portability, you should perform random access operations only on files opened in binary mode. The six functions you're given in Stream I/O to do random access on binary files are these:

read	Read a string of characters from an input stream
write	Write a specified number of characters to an output stream
seekg	Move the position of the file read pointer to a specified offset
tellg	Return the current position of the file read pointer
seekp	Move the position of the file write pointer to a specified offset
tellp	Return the current position of the file write pointer

Take note

This is a *Made Simple* book, and having covered *Made Simple* file access, I must here again refer you to the *Newnes C++ Pocket Book* for explanation and examples of use of these functions.

Exercises

1. Write a program that uses any combination of the width, precision and fill functions to display the number 1.732050808 (square root of 3!) to four decimal places of accuracy, to a total width of not more than 10 characters, right justified and with the leading '1' left-padded with zeros.

2. Write a program that implements a **file** class. Define the file's data and function members. Include a simple **encrypt** function that uses exclusive-or scrambling performed by the single line of code:

   ```
   c ^= key;
   ```

   where **c** is a **int** variable and **key** is either a literal character or a character variable used to scramble **c**.

7 Answers to exercises

Chapter 1

1. Here's a reasonable **car** class declaration, implemented by the instance definition that follows:

    ```
    class car
    {
    private:
        double    weight;
        double    length;
        char      colour[10];
        double    max_speed;
    public:
        bool  start();          // bool return value for success of failure
        void  stop();
        void  accelerate(double  rate);
        void  turn(int lr);     // turn left or right
        void  reverse();
    };

    //  implement with class instance
        car    newcar;
        int    startok;         // true or false

        startok = newcar.start();
    ```

2. If you actually have any savings, you might want to extend the base account class like this:

    ```
    class savings : public cust_acc
    {
    protected:
        double    interest;
        double    int_rate;
    public:
        void      calc_interest();
    };

    //  addition to accfunc.cpp
    void  savings::calc_interest()
    {
        interest = bal * rate/100;
    }
    ```

3. Here's the overloaded += operator, added to the declaration of **cust_acc**:

```
class  cust_acc
{
private:
    float  bal;
    int  acc_num;
public:
    void  setup();
    void  lodge(float);
    void  withdraw(float);
    void  balance();
    void  operator+=(double  amt){bal  +=  amt;}
};

// add a grand to my balance
cust_acc  my_acc;
    ...
my_acc  +=  1000.00;
```

Chapter 2

1. This is the minimal **clock** class, followed by the functions and calls required by the question:

```
class clock
{
private:
    int hours;
    int minutes;
public:
    void   adv_hours();
    void   adv_minutes();
};

//  clockfn.cpp
void  clock::adv_hours()
{
    if (hours < 24)
    {
        hours++;
        minutes=0;
    }
    else
        hours = minutes = 0;
}
void  clock::adv_minutes()
{
    minutes++;
    if (minutes >= 60)
        adv_hours();
}

//  call from external function
clock  wall_clock;
wall_clock.adv_minutes();
```

2. You can't initialise an instance of a C++ class in this way – the way you would initialise a C structure. You should set a class instance to its initial values using a constructor function taking parameters representing the items of data beginning with "**J. Smith**".

3. The **policy** class will contain an extra data member, with **private** access:

```
        static  char  glob_polno[8];
```

The value of **glob_polno** is initialised (once only) by this definition, which must be made outside all functions:

```
char  policy::glob_polno[8]  =  "10000";
```

The **pol_open** function must then set **polno** for the current class instance and assign the next number to **glob_polno**:

```
strcpy(polno,   glob_polno);

char  tmp[8];
sprintf(tmp,  "%s",  atoi(glob_polno)  +  1);
strcpy(glob_polno,   tmp);
```

You can create the two instances of policy with these definitions, setting them up with calls to **pol_open**:

```
policy  mypol,  yourpol;
mypol.pol_open();
yourpol.pol_open();
```

The values of **polno** for the instances **mypol** and **yourpol** are now "**10000**" and "**10001**" respectively.

Chapter 3

1. The four cases of initialisation that invoke a copy constructor are:

   - Creation of a class instance by explicit call to a copy constructor.

   - Creation of a class instance by initialisation using an assignment operator.

   - Creation of a class instance by passing an argument to a function.

   - Creation of a class instance by returning a value from a function.

   Here are short examples:

   ```
   string s1;          // make the first instance of class string

   string s2(s1);      // case 1 above
   string s3 = s2;        // case 2 above
   s4 = func(s3);      // case 3 above

   string func(string s_in)
   {
       return(s_in);   // case 4 above
   }
   ```

2. You can also write the chained overloaded assignment operation like this:

   ```
   s3.operator=(s2.operator=(s1));
   ```

   This shows that the chained overloaded assignment is in fact a series of nested function calls. The call **s2.operator=(s1)** must return the instance **s2** (generated by the **operator=** function returning ***this**) for the function call **s3.operator=**(...) to have an argument.

3. If you got this one right, well done. You had to extrapolate a bit from your knowledge of operator overloading (and maybe read a bit of Chapter 6) to answer this question. Here's the declaration, made in the scope of the declaration of the class **myclass**, of the overloaded function:

   ```
   friend ostream& operator<<(istream&, myclass);
   ```

   and here's the function itself:

```
ostream&  operator<<(ostream&  s,  myclass  inst);
{
    c << inst.datamember << "\n"; // output some member

    return(s);
}
```

To use the new operator <<, newly overloaded to perform stream output for the class **myclass**, we define an instance and then 'send it to **cout**':

```
myclass  inst;
cout << inst; // call to overloaded function.
```

The overloaded function must not be a member of **myclass**, but rather a **friend**. This is because **cout**, rather than an instance of **myclass**, will always appear to the left of the operator. If an overloaded-operator function is a member of a class, then an instance of that class must appear to the left of the operator.

Chapter 4

1. Here are the constructors (written as if they were defined inline within the class declarations) needed for classes **a**, **b** and **c**:

    ```
    a(int i_in) {i = i_in;} // constructor for 'a'

    //  constructor for 'b'
    b(char c_in, int i_in) : a(i_in)
    {
        ch = c_in;
    }

    //  constructor for 'c'
    c(double d_in, char c_in, int i_in) : b(c_in. i_in)
    {
        d = d_in;
    }
    ```

2. First, here's the constructor (written this time as an external definition) for **manager**:

    ```
    manager::manager(double    bonusIn,
              double  payRateIn,
              int  gradeIn,
              int  employeeNoIn,
              char  nameIn[30])
    : employee(gradeIn, employeeNoIn, nameIn)
    {
        bonus = bonusIn;
        payRate = payRateIn;
    }
    ```

    followed by the somewhat simpler base **employee** constructor:

    ```
    employee::employee(int    gradeIn,
              int  employeeNoIn,
              char  nameIn[30])
    {
        grade = gradeIn;
        employeeNo = employeeNoIn;
        strcpy(name,  nameIn);
    }
    ```

Chapter 5

1. This is the class template declaration of the **array** *container class*:

```
template <class arraytype>
class array
{
private:
    int     size;
    arraytype *aptr;
public:
    array(int elements = 1)
    {
        size = elements;
        aptr = new arraytype[elements];
    }
    void fill_array();
    void disp_array();
    ~array() { delete [] aptr; }
};
```

When you instantiate a template class for the **char** type:

```
array<char>   charArray(10);
```

you get an array of ten elements of type **char**. The constructor uses the argument **10** to set the number of elements in the array, while the placeholder **arraytype** is substituted in this case with the **char** parameterised type. If no argument is given for the number of elements, the number is set in the constructor to a default of **1**.

You can do instantiations for **int** and **double** is much the same way:

```
array<int>   intArray(5);
    array<double>   doubleArray(15);
```

Finally, here's how to write externally the definition of one of the class template functions, for example **fill_array**:

```
template <class arraytype>
void   array<arraytype>::fill_array()
{
    for (int i = 0; i < size; i++)
    {
        cout << "Enter data: ";
        cin >> aptr[i];
    }
}
```

2. In answer to this question, we'll declare a class called **anyclass**:

```
class anyclass
{
private:
    // data members defined here
public:
    // function members defined here
    int operator>(anyclass& a2);
};
```

and use instances of it as arbitrary objects for comparison with our template function **max**. The **max** function template looks like this:

```
//   define general template for arbitrary objects
template<class obj>
obj& max(obj& o1, obj& o2)
{
    //   overloaded > used here
    if (o1 > o2)
        return (o1);
    return (o2);
}
```

To use it, we define three instances of **anyclass**:

```
    anyclass a1, a2, a3;

    // set initial values of a1 and a2 here,
    // then instantiate and call a template function
    a3 = max(a1, a2);
```

The **max** template function uses the overloaded > operator. You define the overloading function as follows:

```
//   define overloaded > operator function
int anyclass::operator>(anyclass& a2)
{
    // if a1 greater than a2
        return (1);
    return (0);
}
```

and it's up to you to define what it means to assert that **a1** is greater than **a2**.

Chapter 6

1. Here's the program for formatting **1.732050808**:

```cpp
#include   <iostream.h>

int main()
{
    double  root3 = 1.732050808;

    //    default display is left-justified with precision 6
    cout << root3 << endl;

    //    set precision 4, field width 10 and fill character +
    cout.precision(4);
    cout.width(10);
    cout.fill('0');

    cout << root3 << endl;

    return(0);
}
```

2. And finally, here's my suggested **file** class (there are any number of ways of doing this, many of them good). The file consists of a number of records which, for the sake of illustration, store personal and national insurance details. Because of space considerations, I don't present here the definitions of all the member functions.

```cpp
struct  record
{
    char      fname[15];
    char      lname[15];
    char      city[20];
    char      nat_ins_no[8];
    int       age;
    int       height_cm;
    char      sex;

    void      display_rec();
};

class  file
{
private:
    char      filename[20];
```

```cpp
        ifstream   inp;
        ofstream  outp;
        record    *rec;
        int        no_recs;
        long       start_off;
public:
    file();
    int        read_rec();
    int        position();
    int        write_rec();
    bool       encrypt();
    ~file();
};

bool file::encrypt();
{
    int c;
    int key = 'k';

    inp.open(filename, ios::in | ios::binary);
    outp.open("cipher.dat", ios::out | ios::binary);

    while (inp.get(c), !inp.feof())
    {
        c ^= key;
        outp << c;    // send to 'cipher.dat'
    }
    inp.close();
    outp.close();
}
```

Index